Dedicated to myself,

because I always knew I could do it!

Table of Contents

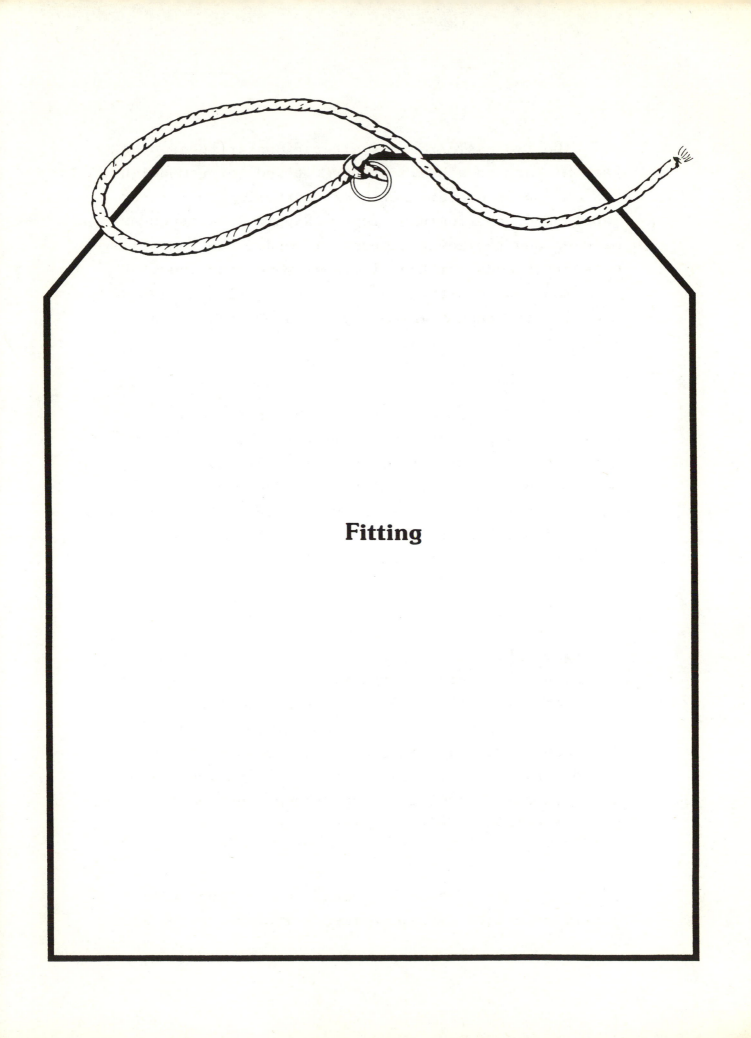

Fitting

The two basic reasons alterations are needed on garments are to achieve proper fit and for remodeling.

Examples of remodeling are narrowing collars or lapels and tapering pant legs. Repair work, such as mending and replacing zippers, is under the remodeling category because fitting is usually not involved.

Most other alterations need to be fitted. There are five components which may be called standards for a good fit, and they are as follows:

1. <u>Ease</u>. This is the extra amount of fullness the designer has put into the garment in addition to the actual body measurements. Ease is what allows us to move comfortably in our clothing. The amount of ease in a garment is of utmost significance in fitting for alterations, because aside from length problems, the customer will most commonly complain of tightness or looseness.

2. <u>Line</u>. Line is composed of three factors which are silhouette, circumference, and design. These are the elements that make up the structure of the garment. Line affects fit most commonly, and usually detrimentally, when the customer purchases a garment whose line is not flattering to her body type. The alterationist can usually make the garment comfortable, but not necessarily flattering.

3. <u>Grain</u>. All fabric has crosswise or lengthwise direction called grain. Garments must be cut on the

grain of the fabric or they will not hang properly.
Most of us have experienced levis that curled around
our legs when worn because they were cut off-grain.
If there is enough extra ease, the alterationist may
be able to correct the problem if it is slight, but
in general, a garment that is cut off-grain cannot
be fixed.

4. <u>Set</u>. Set refers to how the garment hangs on the
body. The alterationist looks for wrinkles in the
fabric which usually point to fitting problems. By
altering the garment, it will fit or "set" properly
on the body. Aside from ease, set is the most important factor in fit.

5. <u>Balance</u>. The proportions of a garment in relation
to the body it is on make up the balance. Hemline
adjustments affect the balance of a garment, as do
straightness of seams and the addition of shoulder
pads. Differences in body types will play havoc with
the balance of a garment and will thus necessitate
alterations.

The sum of these five elements adds up to form
the fit of the garment. As mentioned before, as an
alterationist you will be dealing mainly with ease
and the set of the garment. That is because these are
the two factors which you can usually change after the
garment has been made. Line, grain, and balance are
more important at the time the garment is being ini-
tially constructed.

Any alteration is composed of two parts, each
being of equal importance. They are the fitting and

the actual sewing. Neither can be accomplished properly without the successful execution of the other. Sewing is what usually comes to mind first when thinking of alterations, but no amount of sewing can correct a garment that has not been marked and fitted accurately in the beginning.

Laying the groundwork for a successful fitting will begin before you even see the customer. First of all, arrange your fitting area so it will be of optimum use to you and of optimum comfort to your customer. You must have either a separate dressing room or an area that can be closed off for privacy. Be sure to have hooks and hangers for clothing and a chair or seat. Try to make the space large enough so the customer will not be uncomfortable or inconvenienced while she is changing. Have a clean restroom available. In general, people dislike trying on clothing, so try in every way you can to make it a pleasant experience.

It is very important to have proper lighting and a full-length mirror. It is easy to be tempted to buy a cheaper dimestore mirror but these quite often have ripples or distortions that add bulges right in the wrong places on the customer's body. I have found that it is much better in the long run to invest in a good quality mirror from a glass or specialty store. A three-way mirror is the ideal, but you will be able to do quite well with one floor-length mirror and a hand mirror for rear viewing.

Have measuring tape, yardstick, pins, and marking chalk within arm's length of your mirror so you can fit the garment without stepping away. Don't forget clips, clothespins, or whatever marking devices you use for ultrasuede or leathers which cannot be marked the conventional ways. Pen, paper, order pad, lint brush, and business cards should also be in this immediate area.

Your first contact with a customer may be on the telephone. For this reason, always answer in a businesslike way, such as, "Good morning. This is Always Alterations. How can I help you?" If you are working in a shop, this will become matter of course. If you are working in your home and choose not to install a separate business line, it is very important to have family members understand the necessity of good phone manners. Children in particular will need to be educated to take and receive messages accurately. Help them by practicing what you would like them to say and have a pencil and paper readily available at all extensions.

Quite often customers will be calling to inquire about prices. Before quoting any prices, question the customer thoroughly about the type of job she needs. Gather as many details as possible in order to get a precise picture of what she expects. It is a good idea to give only an estimate on the phone until you can see the project. What is a simple hem to a customer could turn out to be a pair of fully lined pants with top-stitching and ankle zippers that need to be shortened. In a case like this you could say, "A basic hem is $5.00, but there is an extra charge for details such as lining or topstitching." Then, after examining the garment firsthand, you can give a definite price quote.

If you are going to see customers by appointment only, say so from the beginning. You will be communicating the fact that you have other customers, but each will receive your exclusive attention at her allotted time. Tell the customer what she needs to bring to the first appointment, such as the shoes she will be wearing with the garment and the appropriate undergarments. Give specific directions to your place of business and mention any special parking or entrance accommodations. Be sure to get the customer's telephone number. Repeat the appointment time and date if there is one and don't forget a "thank you."

Included in the subject of telephone etiquette is the option of whether or not to use an answering service or answering machine. The biggest argument in favor of either is that your chances of missing potential business calls will be decreased. The biggest negative of a machine is that some people dislike leaving messages on recorders. For this reason, live answering services are sometimes more popular. If you do decide on an answering service or machine, always return calls promptly.

During the initial fitting with the customer, never underestimate the power of a first impression. Even without speaking, many facts can be communicated such as approximate age, nationality, occupation, interests, religion, economic status, and marital status. By simple body language, we convey personality characteristics like patience, assertiveness, shyness, friendliness, cautiousness, and confidence. By observing people's actions, we can tell if they are willing to participate, if they are distracted, or if they are embarrassed. Because of this, always try to make the most of the first impression that your customer receives from you. Since you are working in the clothing profession, the way you dress will be of primary importance.

This does not mean that you have to have an extensive high-fashion wardrobe, but your ability to sew and fit should be evident on you. Your clothing should be clean, becoming, and comfortable. A few well-fitting classic styles will go a lot farther than a closet full of trendy impulse items. Try to convey a courteous but businesslike manner with your speech and gestures. Put yourself in the customer's position and do everything you can to put her at ease. Greet her pleasantly using her name if you know it, and introduce yourself. Show her where to stand, sit, change clothes, put her coat, or wait.

It is not uncommon for a customer to emerge from the dressing room in a garment that appears to need no alteration at all, or in your opinion, needs a completely different alteration from the one the customer desires. From this point on, it is very important to remember that your job is to please the customer. Refrain from statements like, "I see you need this dress shortened," or "It looks like these pants are way too tight." The customer may be quite happy with the length or the tightness and you will only alienate her by disagreeing. Instead, say something like, "Now, how can I help you?", or, "What alteration did you need today?" If you already know that it is a hem that is needed, reconfirm that fact by saying," I understand you need these pants shortened?", or, "I recall from our phone conversation that you need the sides taken in."

During the fitting, you will need to constantly question and instruct the customer. Position her in front of the mirror and ask her to stand on both feet and to look forward. This is necessary because the hem of the garment as well as the general set of the garment will change if she looks down or twists. For a customer who appears nervous or embarrassed, you can "break the ice" by firmly touching her shoulder while positioning her in front of the mirror. Position yourself behind and to one side of the customer and view the garment in the mirror just as she sees it. Explain what you are doing as you go by saying, "I will pin the sides," "I'll mark the hem," or, "Stand still and I will go around you."

You will greatly enhance customer relations by reserving your professional, and personal, opinion until asked for it. Remember, some people prefer clothing tighter or looser than the norm; or, they actually want to wear their pants at a length that you would consider "high waters." Try not to counsel the customer unless you foresee a problem that could arise from her instructions. For example, "I will be glad to take the pants in this much, but I must caution you that it will cause the pockets to gap open," or, "Taking the sides in this much will cause the pockets to gap slightly. Will this be a problem for you?" If a fitting problem is extremely obvious to you and not to the customer, try to mention it very diplomaticly. For instance, "I think if the sleeves were shortened you would be more comfortable and the garment may be in better proportion." Of course, if the customer asks you to recommend what can be done to improve the fit, be sure to give your advice as tactfully and as honestly as possible. When you have clarified what is needed and agreed upon it, you will be able to proceed with optimum effectiveness.

Sometimes a garment will appear to have so many things wrong with it that you will wonder where to start pinning. After making sure the garment is buttoned, snapped, etc., correctly, look for wrinkles. A wrinkle will almost always point directly to where the problem is originating. A general rule is to fit from the top down. On a blouse, dress, or jacket, always check and pin the collar area first. Then proceed to the shoulders, sides, and last of all to the length of the sleeves or hem. With pants, always check and pin the waist and sides first before proceeding to the hem. Any alteration done within the body of the garment will affect the length so it must be pinned first. Sometimes you will find it necessary to sew the alteration in the body of the garment and have the customer return for a fitting on length.

While fitting, ask the customer her preference. Say, "How does that look?", "Do you like it tighter?", or "Shall I make it shorter?" Try to use socially acceptable terms when referring to parts of the body such as hips instead of rear end, apex or point of bust instead of nipple, and bust instead of boobs. Refer to an extra roll of fat as extra width or say, "You are fuller here." Replace skinny with slender or thin. Don't try to avoid a handicap or deformity, for that may be the reason the customer needs your help. On the other hand, try not to be shocked or to stare. Treat it as a part of the whole. Address the problem and go about solving it.

You will come into contact with varied conditions which will make it impossible to complete certain alterations. Try to anticipate these and examine the garment before the customer leaves so she can be informed if this is the case. Usually a garment cannot be altered if the customer has lost more than thirty-five pounds. If the garment is cut off-grain there is nothing that can be done to correct it unless the error is very, very slight. You probably cannot change the line of a garment from one design to another, such as from a dolman sleeve to a set-in sleeve. A big problem , especially with women's clothing, is that there will not be enough seam allowance to let out if needed. Quite often hems cannot be lengthened due to lack of fabric or because the original hemline shows. Sometimes a facing will help or topstitching over the old line will do the trick, but make sure the customer agrees in advance to your method. Inability to match thread, zippers, or other findings is a common dilemma and can inspire creativity. If reweaving is an impossibility, unusual rips and tears will have to be mended as best you can, remembering to inform the customer of the situation.

If your machine simply won't handle leather, vinyl, or other special fabrics, don't take the chance of ruining a garment by trying to force it. Along the same lines, if you come across an alteration that is beyond your skill level at the time, simply state that you do not do that type of alteration. Don't destroy future business by trying and failing, and don't destroy the customer's confidence in you by saying you don't know how. Practice on an old or discarded garment and next time you will be able to accept the job.

Lastly, it is very unhealthy and unpleasant to work on a soiled garment. In fact, some states have laws that garments must be cleaned before they can be altered. An easy way to avoid embarrassing confrontations with customers is to have a simple sign in the dressing room which states, "Please have garments cleaned prior to altering. Thank you!", or, "Thank you for having your garment cleaned prior to altering!"

Before the customer leaves, record as many details as possible on the receipt pad. Get her name, address, and phone number. Describe the garment in writing, such as "navy pleated wool skirt, lined." Record what work is to be done, and note special details like "hand-stitched hem" or "topstitched." Be sure to date the receipt and state your terms for payment so they are understood from the beginning. If you collect a down-payment, calculate the balance. Examine the garment for stains or tears and politely call them to the customer's attention so you will not be held responsible for them later. When the fitting is over, hang the garment neatly rather than leaving it on the floor or over a chair. Give the customer a time estimate for completion or set up the next appointment.

SAMPLE RECEIPT PAD

			101	
PHONE			DATE	
732 - 4571			2/10	
CUSTOMER'S NAME				
Lois Prudhome				
ADDRESS				
455 S.W. Parkview				
City 93420				

QUAN.	DESCRIPTION	PRICE	
1	Navy lined skirt- shorten	$8	50
1	White pants- shorten + topstitch	7	50
		16	00
	down	- 5	00
	due on delivery	11	00

Marking and Sewing

Later in this book, each specific alteration will be outlined in detail, but first I would like to discuss some general guidelines for marking and sewing.

Pins are the most traditional marking implements. Plastic or glass headed pins are by far the most convenient to use and have the added benefit of being easy to see both in the garment and in the carpeting. You may want to keep a small supply of #17 silk pins for use on silk and sheer fabrics. Be sure to buy only rustproof pins which will be brass, nickel-plated steel, or stainless steel. Virtually all pins are stainless steel today, but check the composition of "bargain bin" pins that seem to be a good buy. You will quickly lose the money you saved by ruining one customer's garment with rust spots. If you have never used one, you may want to try using a wrist pin cushion for easy accessibility during fitting.

As you become more experienced in marking, I believe you will come to appreciate the advantages of using tailor's chalk. It will allow you to mark much faster than you can with pins and you will not lose the mark as a result of the pin falling out. Pins are necessary for pinning out excess fabric, but chalk can be used in almost every other situation.

Tailor's chalk comes in thin rectangular cakes of two kinds, the first being composed of a waxlike substance. It is perfect for marking wool, dark fabrics, and some washables like cotton. This type of chalk can be sharpened to a fine point with a razor blade and will enable you to make clear and precise

marks. The mark will vanish with the touch of an
iron. I have seen regular household soap used as a
substitute for tailor's chalk, but it can contain
perfume, dyes, or additives that may discolor the
fabric or burn on the iron after pressing.

The other type of chalk is just like real chalk,
but firmer. It is better for silks, linings, or del-
icate fabrics because it can be brushed off. The wax
chalk will leave a greasy mark when used on these
fabrics. Regular chalkboard chalk can be substituted,
but it does not have a narrow edge and your marks can
become very inaccurate.

Both types of chalk come in a variety of colors,
but I find plain white is the most reliable and stain
proof. They can be found in pencil form or with special holders.

There are distinctive marks made with chalk which
form a universal language among tailors and alterationists. A simple straight broken line means either
"shorten" or "take in." A broken line with slash marks
means "let out" or "lengthen." In the case of taking
in garments (making them smaller) pins are usually used
so the customer can see how the garment will fit.

It is a good idea to make your conversation con-
sistent and explicit by referring to making a garment
smaller as "taking in" and to making a garment larger
as "letting out." For hems, always use "shorten" or
"lengthen" and there will be no mistake as to what is
needed. These are used instead of expressions like
"taking up" which could mean either shortening the hem
or taking the sides in.

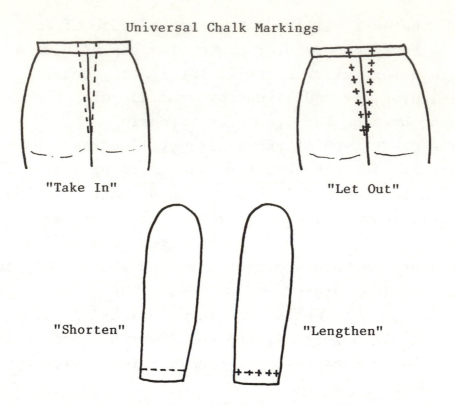

Universal Chalk Markings

"Take In" "Let Out"

"Shorten" "Lengthen"

The use of chalk is also very helpful when trans-
ferring markings from the outside to the inside of the
garment. Let's assume you are taking in the sideseams
of a jacket. You have pinned the seams and now must
transfer your pin marks to the inside so you will be
able to sew.

Jacket Back

The sideseams are
pinned for taking in.

Go to the inside of the garment and make small chalk marks just where the pins are holding the fabric together. Remove the pins and connect the marks forming a solid line. This will signify the new sewing line.

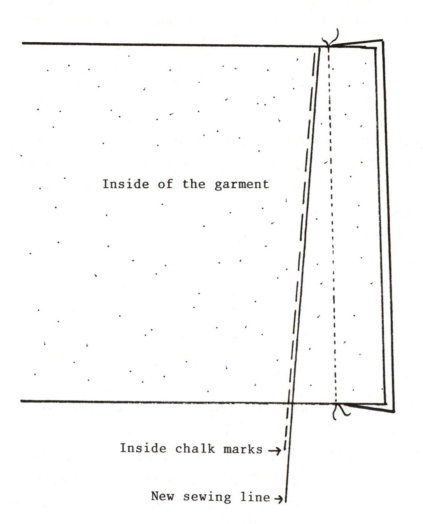

Inside of the garment

Inside chalk marks →

New sewing line →

If there are only chalk marks and no pins on the garment, go to the inside and put chalk marks directly under the ones on the outside. Do this by pressing down on each mark with your finger from the outside and pressing up from the inside with chalk. Connect the marks and sew.

When a garment is pinned on a customer, it won't be as tight as if there were a complete seam sewn. Because of this, always sew on the outside of your new sewing line when taking in. This will guard against "over altering," a common mistake among novice alterationists. In like manner, if you are shortening a pair of pants, always make them a fraction longer than you have marked them because they will "draw up" or shorten slightly as the customer wears them.

Keep other marking implements close at hand, such as yardstick, seam gauge, hem marker, and tape measure. Don't forget to have clips or clothespins for special fabrics such as ultrasuede or leather. There are really no "proper" marking devices except those that seem to work the best for you. Many "new fangled" products hold a big attraction but I find the best policy is to go with versatility and simplicity. For instance, there is a whole barrage of new air-sensitive, water-sensitive, etc., marking pens in the stores. They are quite expensive compared to pins or chalk and you will find yourself with a real problem when they dry up!

After we have fitted, marked, and sewn, the time comes for ripping out. I often hear the common complaint, "If it weren't for the ripping out, I'd love to sew!" My answer is, "Learn an easy way to rip out!" Traditional seam rippers are never used in tailoring shops but are replaced most commonly by single-edged razor blades and sometimes by small pocket knives. Using a sharp razor blade or knife appears to be much riskier than using a seam ripper but in actuality it is not. How many times have you torn

the fabric or cut your hand by trying to force a dull
seam ripper? All you need is practice (on a garment
other than the customer's) and I am sure you will be
amazed at the speed you will develop in ripping. In-
cidentally, the best place to buy razor blades in
bulk is at a home improvement or paint store.

Try to take advantage of chain stitches and
blindhem stitches which are sewn with one or two continuous threads. They will always rip out quickly
by clipping a few threads and pulling from left to
right. In general, <u>always sew the new seam before
ripping out the old one</u>. The old seam will serve as
basting or pinning while you're sewing the new one.

*Note: The wrong side of fabric in all illustrations
will be dotted.

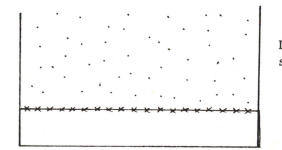

Dots signify wrong
side of fabric.

This hem is turned
up and stitched.

Garment inside.

19

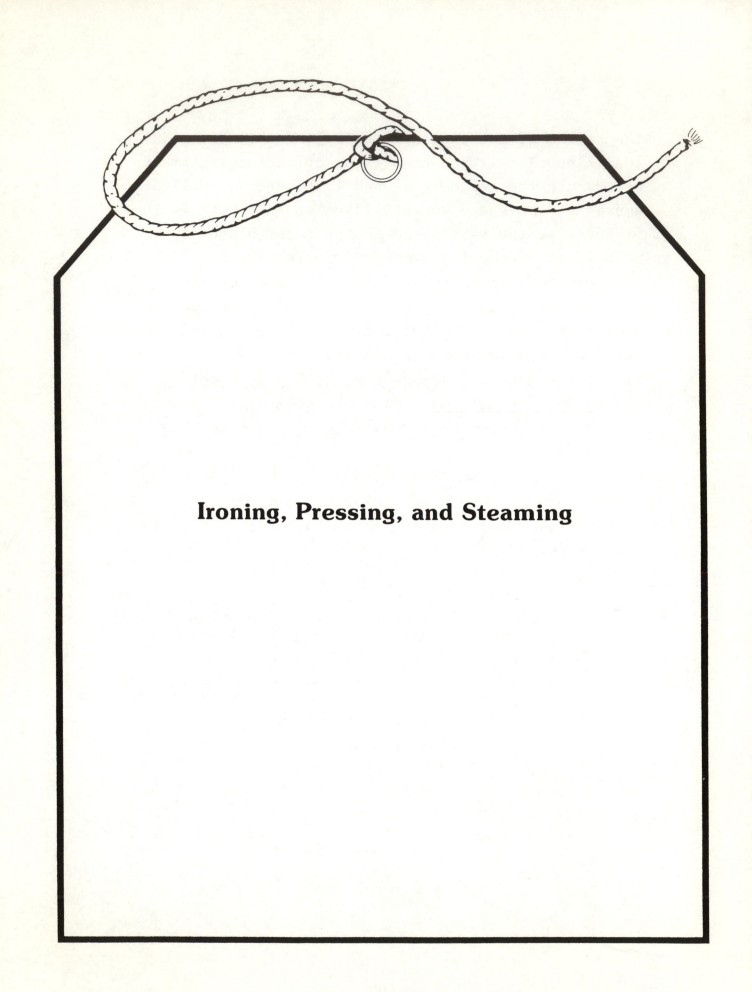

Ironing, Pressing, and Steaming

Ironing the customer's garment will be much easier if you use a pressing table instead of an ironing board. The ideal table can be made cheaply by padding and covering a door and positioning it on a table, dresser, bookcases, or other sturdy support. The stability and added surface size will give you the strength you need for pressing and the area you need for the garment, iron, and other accessories. If you don't have enough space for a whole door, cover and pad as large a board as possible.

Your pressing area should include a sleeve board, squirt bottle, and extra press cloths. A tailor's ham is good for pressing large curved areas and a seam roll is used for pressing seams that might leave a mark on the right side of the garment. I find that putting heavy brown paper under the seam allowances works well for this also. There are always areas that these commercial pressing aids don't fit into, so I keep a towel handy and fold it to fit the specific area. A tailor's clapper or pounding block is used to clap or pound the steam out of an area you have just pressed. It is held in place until the area is cooled, thus setting the press.

I'm not going to go into detail about different brands of irons or pressing machines because a normal household iron, if used properly, can perform most tasks needed in doing alterations. Once you have mastered the use of a regular iron, you will be able to shop for complicated equipment.

Ironing

Your iron and the way it is used will be second only to your sewing machine in importance when you are performing an alteration. You will need to distinguish between its three main functions: ironing, pressing, and steaming, and learn to use each appropriately.

Ironing is the process we most commonly use an iron for and its purpose is to remove wrinkles from entire garments or from large areas within a garment. It can be done with a dry iron or with steam. A minimum of pressure is used and the iron is slid back and forth. To avoid wrinkling during the process, iron detailed areas first and then the larger areas.

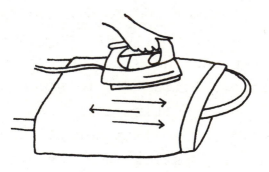

Move the iron back and forth and apply light pressure. Use a dry iron or steam, medium heat.

Pressing

    Pressing differs in that we apply heat, moisture,
and pressure to small areas of a garment at a time
and then move the iron to another area without slid-
ing it. Pressing allows us to mold, shape, and permanently set parts of the garment in place. Because
the iron is put directly on the fabric and force is
applied, use a press cloth unless you have tested the
fabric beforehand. A teflon plate cover can be an
alternative to a press cloth. Always allow garments
and garment parts to cool in the position in which
they were pressed. It is the same principle used in
electric rollers for hair. We use heat, pressure,
and moisture, allow the pressed area to become cool
and dry, and the press is set.

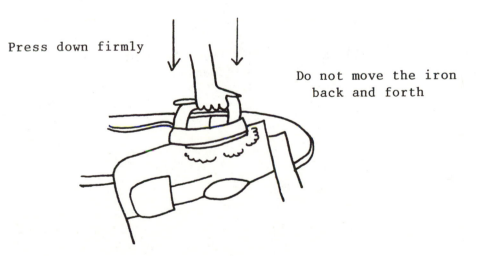

Press down firmly

Do not move the iron
back and forth

Use heat and moisture

Steaming

Steaming is done by holding the iron away from the fabric and allowing the steam to penetrate the garment. This process is used to ease or shrink fabric into the shape we want, or to remove wrinkles from napped fabrics, and to restore the nap if it has been flattened. A shot-of-steam iron works well for steaming because the flow of steam can be regulated.

Hold the iron away from the fabric and
use steam

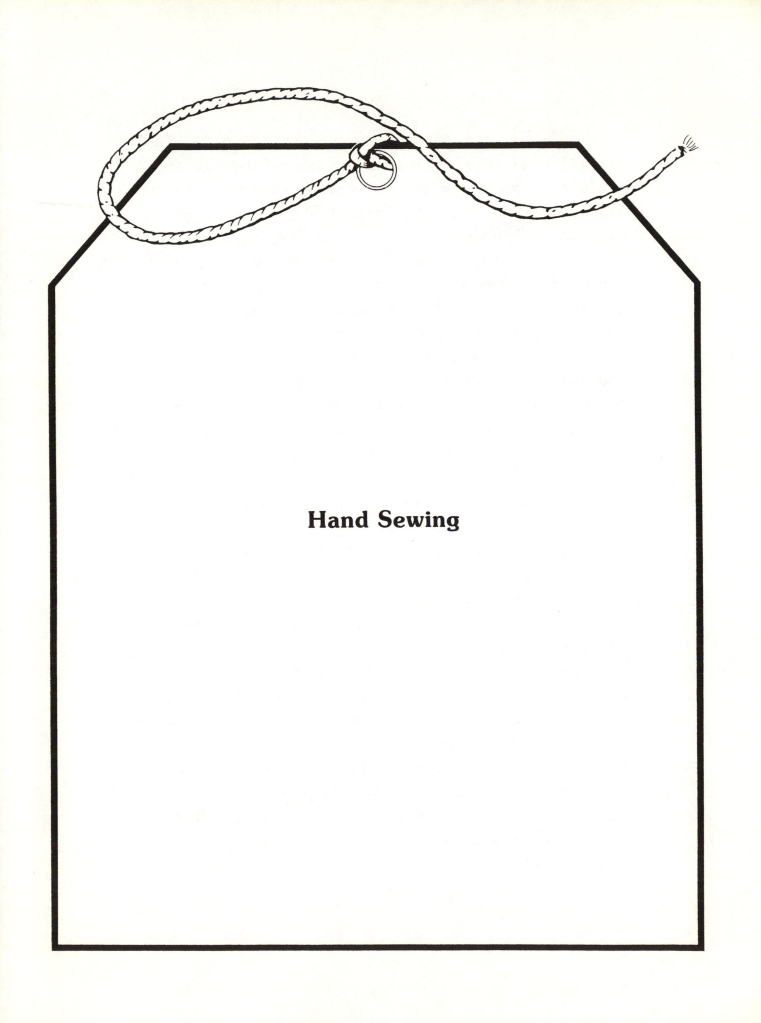

Hand Sewing

Any handwork means time, and your job as alterationist will be to eliminate as much handwork as possible from your sewing. If you do not own a blind-
hemming machine yet, the majority of your handwork
will be on hems.

Needles for handsewing come in a variety of types,
the most common being sharps. They are of medium
length and have small, rounded eyes. Betweens, used
for very detailed work, are shorter; and milliner's
needles, usually used for basting, are the longest
and thinnest. Needle sizes range from one to twenty-
four and I recommend a size seven sharp for general
purpose handsewing. Again, the best thing to do is
to experiment to find the size which is easiest for
you to use.

Silk thread is the easiest thread to use for
handsewing but its cost and availability can be a
problem. Coating regular thread with beeswax will
reduce tangling and knotting and will increase strength.
Simply thread your needle and pull the thread through
the cake of beeswax. The only caution here is that
after pressing the beeswax may leave stains on silky
fabrics. Prewaxed silk finishing thread is the ulti-
mate thread for handsewing and is available in tailor
supply stores. The disadvantage is that it comes only
in several basic colors.

Basting thread, used only for that purpose, is
worth the investment for the few times you will use it.
It is usually white, very wirey, and nearly impossible
to tangle so you can use it in very long pieces. I
have found I can reuse lengths of it several times.

With all thread, knot the end you cut. This will enable you to sew in the direction the thread is twisted and will help eliminate tangles. An eighteen to twenty-four inch strand of thread is the usual length for handsewing.

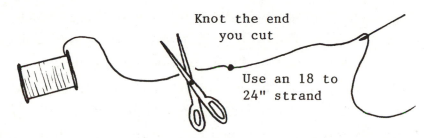

If you are doing a lot of handsewing, you will want to use a thimble. Thimbles can be closed or open on the end. It is generally thought that tailors prefer open-ended thimbles because the stitches they use are pushed from the side of the finger. In like manner, seamstresses use closed-ended thimbles because their stitches require pushing from the top of the finger.

I prefer an open-ended thimble simply because it is cooler. Many sewers praise the leather thimble for comfort. Here again, the type you choose will be will be mostly up to personal preference.

 Close-ended
thimble

Open-ended
thimble

Following are directions for the most common hand stitches you will need to use as an alterationist.

Basting

Basting is a temporary stitch used to hold alterations in place for a second or final fitting. Basting is better than pinning after the first fitting because it will allow the garment a smooth finish and the customer will not be stuck with pins when she views the garment. Basting is usually done on a flat surface and with a thread length longer than the norm. Start with one or two small backstitches instead of a knot and continue with a long running stitch going in and out of the fabric at one half inch intervals. A knot is not used so the basting can be easily removed if needed.

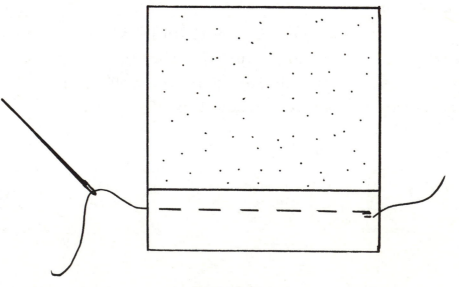

Basted hem

Running Stitch

A running stitch is a stitch similar to basting, only smaller and permanent. A running stitch is used most commonly for tacking lining to the bottom of jacket sleeves or hems and for tacking down facing. Sewing from right to left, use a regular length of thread with a knot and a small stitch, about one fourth inch or less. Weave back and forth catching the lining and then the hem. Make sure the stitch does not show on the outside of the garment.

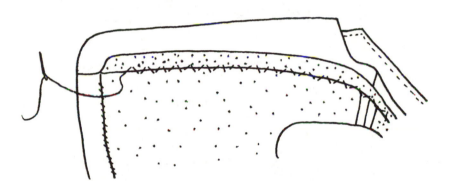

Tacking jacket facing

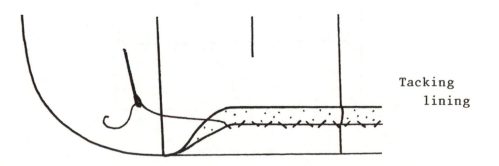

Tacking
lining

Catch and Whip Stitches

Many people prefer to hem with the running stitch. I find that either the catch stitch or the whip stitch is easier and more durable. Use a regular length of thread and a knot for both. Keep your stitches small, just under one fourth inch, and firm, but not tight. Check to see that they are invisible on the outside of the garment.

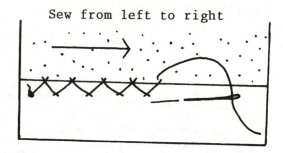

Sew from left to right

CATCH STITCH

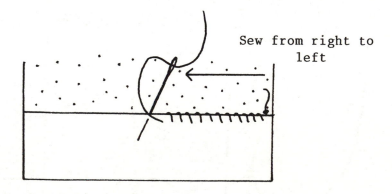

Sew from right to left

WHIP STITCH

Prick Stitch

The prick stitch is sometimes referred to as the pick stitch and is used mostly for applying zippers by hand (called a hand picked zipper). It is used mostly for decorative purposes and usually in tailored garments. You will be surprised how easy it is to apply a zipper using this stitch. You will see this stitch done with a single thread but I prefer to use a double thread for strength. This is a variation of a back stitch and only small dots of thread will be seen on the outside of the fabric. Working on the right side of the fabric, come from the wrong side up through the fabric and zipper to the right side. Go back about two or three threads and enter going through all the layers. Come up a little less than one fourth inch ahead. Keep the stitches very even and the line straight. If this is difficult, make a line with tailor's chalk first for a guide.

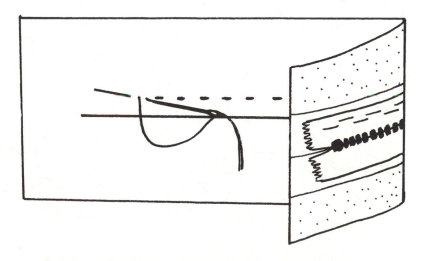

Prick stitch used for zipper application

31

Thread Chain or Tailor's Tack

From time to time you will need to replace thread
beltloops or tailor's tacks on garments. These thread
chains are also used with a snap on the end for lingerie straps. Use a double thread, well waxed, and
with a good knot. Come from underneath and take a few
small reinforcement stitches. Hold the needle and
thread in your right hand. Put your thumb and first
two fingers through the loop and pull a loop through
the first loop, tightening it as you go. After making
the desired length, put the needle through the last
loop to form a knot. Secure the end with several small
stitches and a knot.

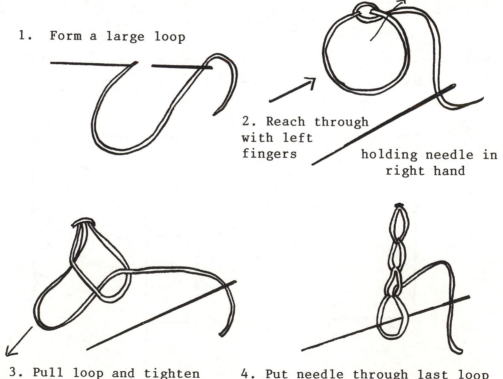

1. Form a large loop

2. Reach through
with left
fingers
      holding needle in
right hand

3. Pull loop and tighten

4. Put needle through last loop
to form knot

Buttons

Under the category of handsewing, I would like to review the steps in sewing a button on because they are so important, and because you will be asked to do this seemingly simple job many times. Buttons for blouses, shirts, and dresses are sewn on with a beeswax reinforced double strand of regular thread. Increase to buttonhole twist, heavy duty thread, or carpet thread for pants, suits, and coats.

Every button, except decorative ones, _must_ have a shank for strength and to work properly. If the button does not have a built-in shank, you can form one easily by putting a needle, toothpick, or match on top of the button and sewing over it. After you have removed the aid, wind the thread around the shank several times and tie off. Even the button on a sheer silk blouse needs a small shank. Try not to cut corners by applying buttons on the machine. You cannot properly form a shank this way and the stitching almost always unravels.

Toothpick used as an aid to
form shank

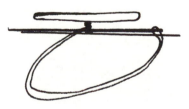

After removing toothpick, wind
thread around shank and knot

Alterations

It is now time to turn to instructions for each individual alteration. I have tried to include every common alteration as well as some that are not so common. No matter how inclusive the list, there will always be some new style or construction method which you will have to figure out yourself. This is when you will use the garment itself for your teacher. Examine how it was sewn originally and put it back together the same way. Do this by taking notes if necessary. Also, do one side at a time. Then you will have the undone side to refer to.

Sometimes, because you have no choice, you will have to develop your own procedure. In this case, try not to slash or trim your seam allowances or hems until you are sure the alteration is fitted properly. If you have to trim fabric in order for the garment to lay properly, such as when mitering corners, be sure the customer knows in advance that the alteration is irreversible. The ability to be flexible and creative is what makes a good alterationist.

"BUT I ONLY HAVE ENOUGH FOOD FOR 2 WEEKS!!"

Pant Alterations

Pant Hems

The length of pant hemlines will ultimately be up to the customer's personal preference. However, you will need to keep abreast of current styles and traditional ones so you can offer advice if asked.

In general, the narrower the pant leg, the shorter the length must be because the hem is not wide enough to fall over the foot and shoe. Very narrow pant bottoms are considered trendy and thus seen almost exclusively in leisurewear. A hemline narrower than 6" usually necessitates the use of a zipper in the seam so the foot can pass through. Because of its narrowness, a 6" hemline could not fall below the ankle, and indeed may be too narrow for some women to wear because of the size of their ankles.

An average width for business or dress pants is 8 to 9". This width allows the pant hem to cover the ankle and part of the top of the shoe. The ideal length for this width of hem has a slight break in front and tapers down ¼ to ½" at the heel. Any width over 10" is considered bell-bottomed and is currently out of fashion.

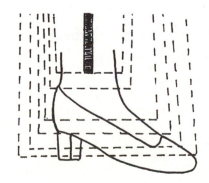

Dotted lines show hemlines from 6" with zipper, 7", 8", 9", 10", and 11" at the bottom.

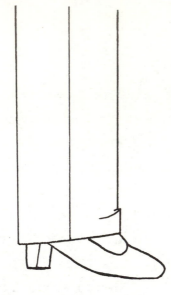

The hem has a slight
break in front and tapers
down in the back.

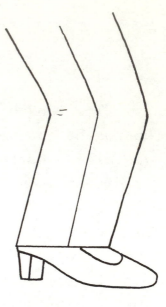

When the knee is bent, as in
walking, the break vanishes.

Armed with this information, you will be able to
advise the customer if she cannot decide on length.
First ask if the customer prefers a slight break or
if she wants the pants to just touch the top of the
shoe.

I recommend pinning the hem so the customer can
see the results. ALWAYS pin or mark both legs. Ev-
eryone has a slight difference in the length of their
legs, and some can vary as much as 1½".

After pinning, reinforce the marks with chalk so
they won't be lost if the pins fall out. Even though
cuffs are generally out of fashion now, ask her if
she wants cuffs or plain bottoms.

Plain Bottomed Hem

1. Remove the old hem.

2. Lay the pants out flat and draw a chalk line from the front chalk mark to the back chalk mark.

Be sure the back mark is at least ¼" lower than the front mark. This causes what is called a "tip" on the hem and makes the hem more pleasing to the eye. If the difference is more than ½", bring it up to ½". Otherwise the tip will appear to be out of proportion.

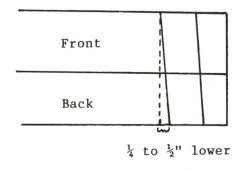

¼ to ½" lower

Draw the new hemline.

3. Measure the hem length and cut off the excess. Commercial hems are usually 1¼ to 1½". This is done to save fabric. I recommend using 2¼ to 2½" as your hem length and the pants will fall better.

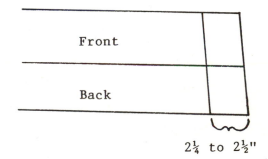

2¼ to 2½"

Cut off the excess.

4. Finish the raw edge. If the original hem was taped, remove the old tape and re-place it. Otherwise, serging is an excellent seam finish. I would zig-zag as a last resort and never pink a woman's hem.

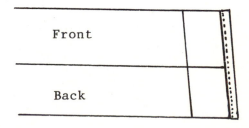

Finish with seam tape or serge.

5. Fold the hem under and press.

6. Sew the hem using a blindhemmer or refer to the hand stitch directions in the "Hand Sewing" section.

7. Depending on the amount of tip, the turned up hem may not seem to fit the pant. It will be too tight in the front and too large in the back if the tip is over ¼".

Allow the hem to lie flat by taking a tuck in the center of the back hem and by opening the sideseams slightly to make extra ease for the front. Take a few tiny hand stitches to tack down the partially opened sideseams.

8. Press the finished hem.

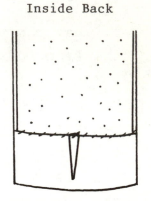

Inside Back

Tuck in hem

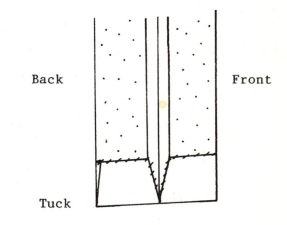

Back   Front

Tuck

Partially opened sideseam

Cuffs

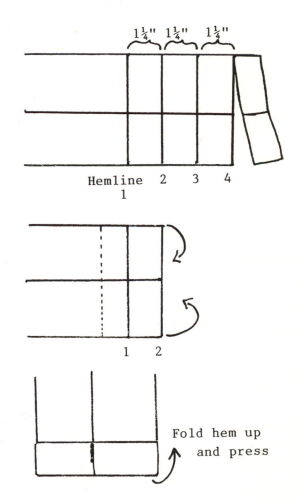

1½
1½
1½
———
4½

1. Mark the hem front and back and ask the customer
what width cuff she wants. (1¼" is the average.) Be
sure to see if there is enough fabric. You will need
3 times the cuff width. For a 1¼" cuff, that would be
3 3/4" past where the hemline is.

2. Draw the hemline. Do
not tip more than ¼" or you
will not be able to make the
cuff lie smoothly.

1¼" 1¼" 1¼"

Hemline 2   3   4
   1

3. Draw 3 more lines the width
of the cuff.

4. Cut off on the last line.
Turn the raw edge under ¼"
and press or stitch to hold
it.

5. Fold the hem under at
the second line and stitch
through the ¼" turnunder.

1   2

6. Fold the cuff up on the
hemline and press.

Fold hem up
and press

7. Tack the cuff in place
by stitching the ditch in
the sideseam and inseam.

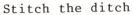

Stitch the ditch

Lining

If the pants are lined, shorten the lining the
same amount as you shorten the pants. Tack it to the
pants in the same way it was originally done.

Levi Hems

Sewing levi hems is always traumatic because of
snapping needles and trying to match topstitching
thread.

Change to a heavy duty needle or try a leather
needle. I usually expect to break at least one needle
sewing a denim hem so I charge a little extra for levis.

After marking, rolling up the hem and pressing,
try giving the thick folds of fabric at the seams a few
hits with a hammer. Be sure to have a solid surface
underneath.

If you cannot find heavy duty thread to match, try
using two threads in the top and one bobbin thread.
If you do this, you will have to sew on the outside of
the garment so the double thread will be outside where
you want it to show.

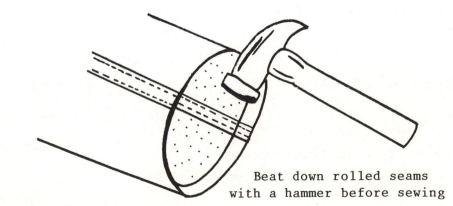

Beat down rolled seams
with a hammer before sewing

Lengthening

Lengthening pants poses two problems. First, there may not be enough fabric to leave a wide enough hem. In this case, you will use purchased hem tape for a facing or you can make your own. If you make your own, it will be much easier to work with if you cut it on the bias. The most important thing to remember is not to stretch the facing while you're sewing it on. After you have applied it, press it. Then press the hem up and proceed as for a normal hem.

The second problem you may have to deal with is that the old hemline may show. If the line is not soiled, squirt water directly on it and press with a cloth. On light colors, you can also try putting diluted white vinegar on the crease and pressing. I am generally unsuccessful at using spot removers when the line is discolored because the stain is usually well set. I find that if the customer is willing, topstitching over the old hemline is a good disguise.

Pants with Zippers in the Hemline

With the physical fitness craze have come sweatpants with zippers at the hem. If the pants need to be shortened more than 1½", you should move the zipper up the same amount the pants are being shortened. Otherwise, you will probably be able to cut the zipper off at the bottom. Just remember to fold the ends under and topstitch several times since you will be cutting off the zipper stop.

Taking In

Sometimes the pants will fit everywhere but at the sideseams. Usually the customer will explain that all she wants is to have the sideseams taken in. This may be because the customer's hips are not as rounded as the pant sideseams or the customer simply wants a tighter fit.

1. Pin the sideseams so the customer can assess the fit.

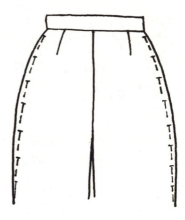

Pants Front

2. Transfer markings to the inside. (Refer to the "Marking and Sewing" section to review transfer of markings.) Connect them with a smooth line and sew. If you are tapering to nothing at the waistband, you will need to remove the waistband at the top of the sideseams so you can sew all the way to the edge of the seam allowance.

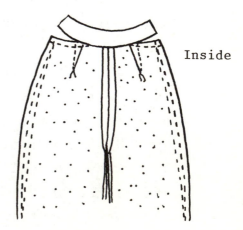

Inside

The waistband is ripped from the pants at the sideseams so the seams can be taken in as marked.

3. Rip out the old seam-
line, trimming if needed,
and press seams open.

4. Resew the waistband.
Be sure to alter the lining
too if there is one.

5. If the customer wants
the sideseams taken in farther down than halfway
through the thigh, you must
then taper the lower legs
(take the amount equally
out of each side) or the
crease will pull to one
side. (Refer to the "Ta-
pering Pant Legs" altera-
tion for instructions.)

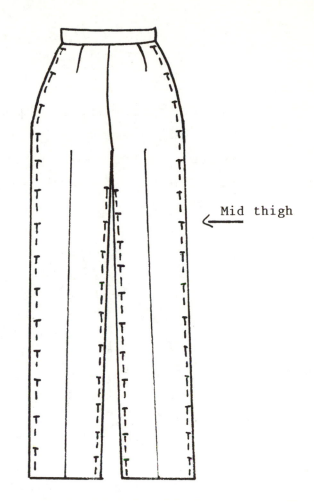

Mid thigh

If the pants have pockets in the sideseams, you
will have two options. First ask if the customer wants
to keep the pockets. If she doesn't care, remove the
pockets and deal with the seam as usual.

If the customer wants to keep the pockets, or if
they cannot be removed because of the design, you will
have to redo the pockets along with taking in the sideseams. Complete one side first and then proceed to
the other so you will always have one finished side to
refer to.

Since this is a very time-consuming process, give
the customer a price quote first so she can decide if
she wants to invest that amount.

If the sideseams have pockets which are simply in-
serted in the seam, you can
take in the sides without
redoing the pockets.

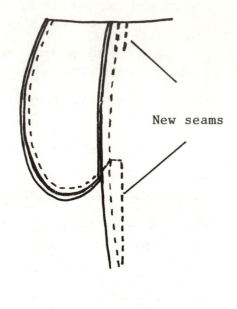

New seams

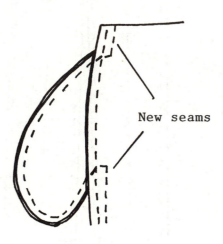

New seams

Below are some examples of pockets which must be removed before the sideseams can be taken in. After
the sides are taken in, the pockets and their facings
are replaced in the new sideseams.

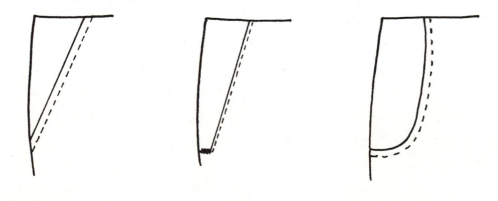

Letting Out Sideseams

Women's clothing rarely has more than 5/8" seam allowances. If you need to let out the sideseams, you must never leave less than ¼". If the seam allowance is this small, stitch the seam twice to reinforce it.

If there are pockets in the sideseams, they cannot be let out. If the customer is desperate, you may be able to let out the back sideseam only, allowing the pocket to remain intact. Here, again, a price quote beforehand is advisable.

The two horizontal marks show where the alteration starts and stops. The diagonal slashes through the sideseam mean "let out all possible."

Use regular "let out" marks if you are marking a specific amount.

Taking in the Waist and/or Seat

Next to hemming, taking in the waist will be your most asked-for pant alteration. When fitting, pinch out the excess fabric at the CB seam. Always ask, "How does that feel?", or, "Do you like the waist on the loose side, tight side, or just normal?" Personal preference is a large consideration in this alteration, so be sure to ask.

Taking in at CB

1. Pin the waist and taper as far down the CB seam as needed. Sometimes the waistband will be so thick, you will not be able to use a pin. In this case, pinch the waist and mark with chalk. If you have pinned, I recommend removing the pins and making chalk marks after the customer has approved the fit. The pins can easily fall out as the customer removes the pants, and your marks will be lost unless you have used chalk.

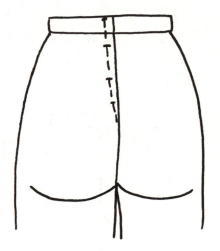

Waist and seat are pinned.

Remove the pins and chalk.

2. It is very common to
take in the waist through
the seat. If this is what
you need to do, pin as before to get the fit, and
replace the pins with chalk
marks.

3. It is extremely important with the seat alteration to get a smooth CB
seam and seat curve.

Transfer your markings to the inside and connect
them to form a good curve. You may have to deviate
from your markings in the seat area slightly to form
this curve properly. There is no set curve formation,
but with experience you will learn what works and what
doesn't.

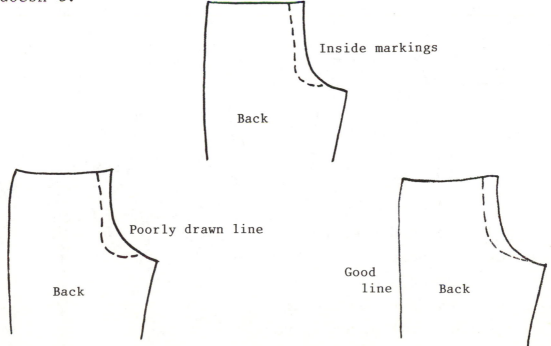

Inside markings

Back

Poorly drawn line

Back

Good
line   Back

4. After you have drawn your new sewing line, always stitch over it twice because of the heavy stress area it is in.

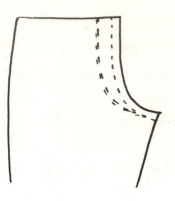

Draw the new line and stitch twice.

5. Remove the old seam and trim leaving at least 1" seams in the waist area and at least 5/8" seams in the seat. Press the seam open down to where the seat curves and leave it closed through the crotch.

Trim the excess.

Press the seam open down to the seat curve and leave it closed through the crotch.

The seat is marked for taking in.

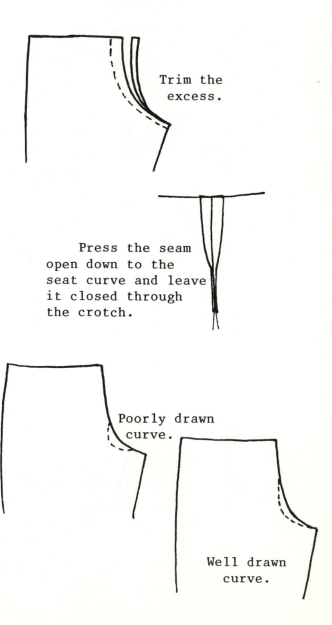

Poorly drawn curve.

Well drawn curve.

6. Once in a great while, you will need to take in the seat only. Pin and chalk as above. Here again, a smooth seat curve is very important.

Removing the Waistband and Taking in the Sides

1. If pinning through the
CB seam and seat still leaves
excess fabric on the sides
of the pants, you may need to
remove and shorten the waistband and take in the sideseams instead.

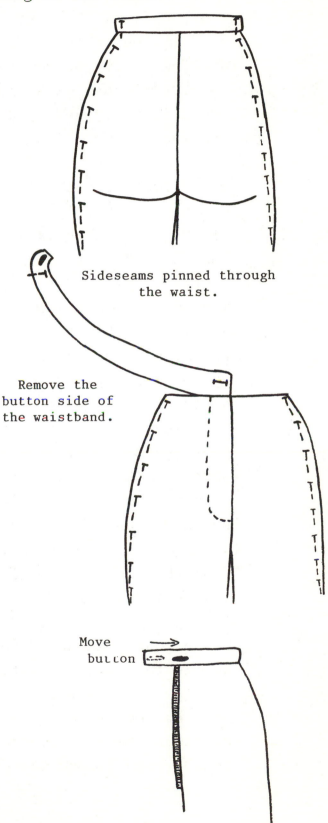

Sideseams pinned through
the waist.

2. Measure the amount to be
removed from the waist and
rip off the waistband all a-
round except on the front
side with the buttonhole.

Remove the
button side of
the waistband.

3. Transfer marks from sideseams to inside and take in,
remembering to draw a smooth
line tapering to nothing.

4. Reapply the waistband and
move the button over the a-
mount you took the waist in
so it will match the buttonhole. You may need to move
belt loops if there are any.

Move
button

Taking in the Waist and/or Seat on Levis

Taking in the waist and/or seat on levis can be difficult for two reasons. First, all the seams are double stitched with special thread, and secondly, the denim is heavy and hard to maneuver in a regular sewing machine.

Many times, especially when women buy men's levis, they will fit in the hips and "pooch out" in the waist. If the levis need to be taken in only in the waist, you may be able to take two darts, one on each side of the back waist. Make the darts about 3 to 3½" long, tapering to nothing just above the pockets. Sew right through the waistband and seam that connects it to the pants. Press the darts toward the CB seam and stitch down through the topstitching on the waistband.

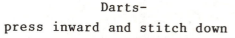

Darts-
press inward and stitch down

If the waist needs to be taken in through the seat, you will need to remove the fabric at the CB seam. This is difficult because of the double topstitched CB seam.

1. First, mark the alter-
ation line with chalk.

2. Remove the belt loop
and waistband at CB. Re-
move the topstitching on the
waistband around the area
where you'll be working.

3. Since there is no CB
seam in the waistband, you
will have to cut through the
waistband to make one and
take out the amount needed.

4. The easiest way to take
in the CB seam is to remove
both rows of topstitching
all the way to the crotch.
You will have to rip the
pant inseams open slightly
so you can remove all the
topstitching. Then take in
the seam as if it were a
normal seam.

5. Trim and finish the raw
edges well because denim
ravels easily. If the customer insists on a double
topstitched seam, simply
turn both seam allowances
to one side and topstitch.

Mark the alteration line
with chalk.

Remove the waistband and
cut through it at the CB
in order to make a seam.

6. If topstitching is not mandatory, leave the seam plain and resew the crotch seam. Reapply the waistband and belt loop.

If you can't find heavy duty topstitching thread to match, try using two spools of regular thread on top and one strand in the bobbin.

Do not retopstitch the CB seam unless it is requested.

" SHE ONLY WEARS DESIGNER BRANDS! "

54

Dropping the Waistband

This alteration is needed when the crotch depth on the pants is too long. An extra fold of fabric may occur right below the waistband and thus denote the amount needed to be removed, or the customer will say that the pants are too "long waisted" or that they "feel baggy in the crotch." Usually the waistband will need to be dropped all around, but occasionally only the front or back will need the alteration.

1. Pin out or chalk the ridge of extra fabric just under the waistband.

Front

2. Measure the amount folded out and mark the new sewing line on the pants.

The new sewing line.

If only the front or back
needs to be dropped, taper
the new sewing line to
nothing a few inches past
the sideseams.

Marks indicate only the front
needs to be dropped.

3. Remove the waistband,
being sure to mark where it
was attached to the CF, CB,
and sideseams.

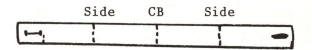

Put markings on the
waistband to indicate where
it is attached to the pants.

4. If there is a zipper in
the pants, and the waistband
is dropped more than 1", you
must move the zipper down before reapplying the waistband.

Take in the sideseams if
the fullness cannot be
eased into the waistband.

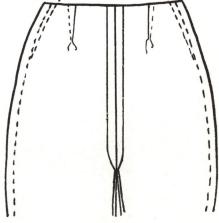

5. Resew the waistband, remembering that the pants should
be at least ½" wider than the
waistband. This extra width
must be eased in and will con-
tribute to a proper fit. Run
a basting stitch on the new
sewing line to help the easing
process. If there is more
than 1" of ease, taper some
width out of the sideseams
so the waistband will fit.

Flat Seat and/or Back Thighs

Need for this alteration is characterized by bagginess in the back of the thighs, or bagginess in the
seat and back of the thighs. Because women's bodies
are shaped in so many different ways, such as with
rounded hips, flat seats, etc., you may need to try
several different fitting methods before you find the
right one to correct the problem.

1. If the pants appear baggy in the seat and back of
the thighs, first pin as for
dropping the back waistband.
You may also need to pin in
the seat.

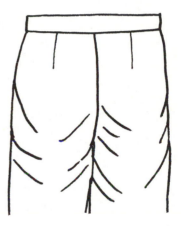

Pants Back

2. Drop the waistband and/or
take in the seat as needed.
(Refer to prior directions
for these two alterations.)

Pants are
pinned for
taking in
the seat and
dropping the
waistband.

3. If you pin the seat and can't seem to pin out enough, pin a fold on the side of each buttock down to the top of the thigh. Pin fabric out of the pants back only.

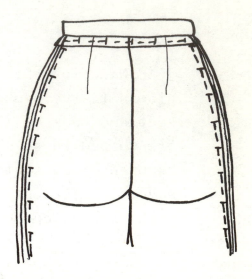

Excess at the sideseams is pinned out of the back only.

4. Remove this amount from the pants back only.

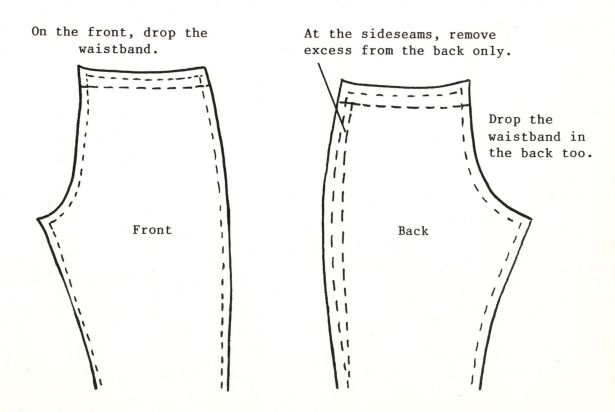

On the front, drop the waistband.

Front

At the sideseams, remove excess from the back only.

Drop the waistband in the back too.

Back

Waist, Seat, and Stride

Taking in the Stride or Waist, Seat, and Stride

This is an advanced alteration both in concept
and technique, and as a result, is widely unknown
among alterationists. This is a standard alteration
for menswear because men do not have the hip curves
that women have. This alteration works well to correct bagginess in the seat and back of the thighs as
a result of weight loss. It differs from the alteration for flat seat and back thighs in that the stride
alteration is more major. Because the customer has
lost weight, the waist will usually be too big also.

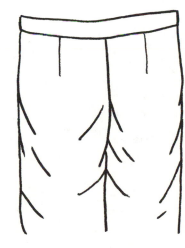

Waist hangs down

Seat and backs of thighs
are baggy

1. Remembering to fit from
the top down, first pin the
waist. It will be pinned so
the pants will be held in
place on the waist properly.

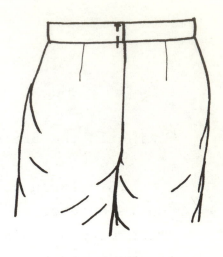

2. Next pinch a horizontal
fold of fabric out of the
CB seam. Pinch enough so
the seam does not hang
loosely on the seat anymore.

3. Make two chalk marks to
signify the width of the
pinch and remove the pin.

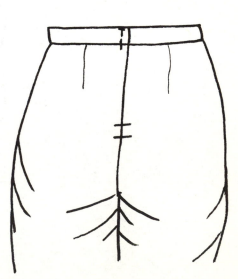

4. Now pin all the way from
the waist through the seat
as far as is needed. Disre-
gard bagginess in the thighs.
(If the customer has lost
35 pounds or more, the pants
cannot be altered enough to
fit properly. Better to
buy a new garment in the
correct size.)

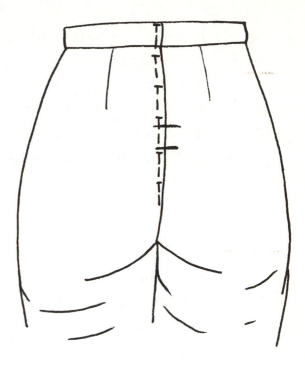

5. Taking in the stride is
another way of saying that
you are removing bagginess
from the back of the thighs.
Go back to the pinch you
took out of the CB seam and
measure it. This will be the
amount to be removed from the
stride.

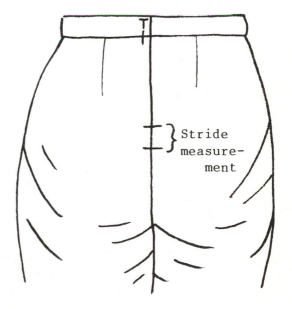

Stride
measure-
ment

6. On the outside of the pants back, start at the bottom of the crotch line starting with the stride measurement. Taper to nothing just below the knee.

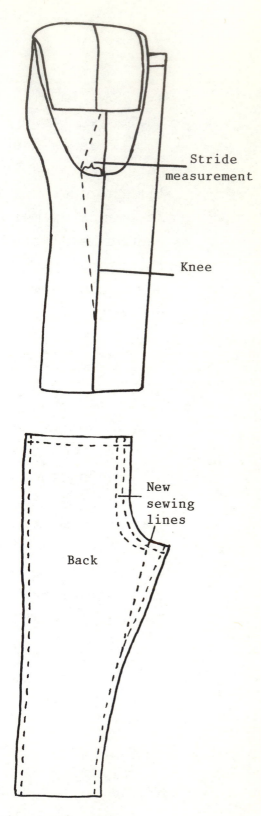

Stride measurement

Knee

7. Rip the lower crotch seam and the leg seam and remove the amount marked from the back pant leg only. This removes the extra fabric from the back of the thigh. If you remove more than 1½", trim some of the seam allowance, but leave at least 1".

New sewing lines

Back

8. Next, take in the waist and seat as described earlier.

9. Taking in the stride will cause the back crease to move inward. Lay the pants out and press in a new back crease from just below the knee up.

Letting Out the Waist, Seat, and Stride

If the customer has gained weight, she will need to have her pants let out in the waist and/or seat, and stride. Before she even tries the garment on, examine the inside to see if there is any seam allowance. A common problem with women's clothing is that there will not be enough to let out, so sometimes all you can do is to "let out all possible."

1. If there is enough seam allowance, you can determine how much to let the waist out in two ways. First, measure the person's waist and then the pants to find the difference.

Measure the customer's waist and then measure the

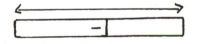

waistband on the inside.

2. Secondly, always have the customer try the pants on. Unbutton the pants in front and unzip slightly. Measure the amount of gap in the open waistband and make a chalk mark on the seam where the pants stop straining.

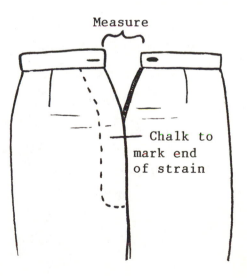

Partially unzip pants that are too tight at the waist.

3. Transfer this chalk mark
to the back to show how far
down the seam needs to be
let out.

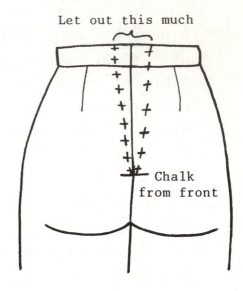

Let out this much

Chalk
from front

Usually if the waist is let
out more than 1", the seat
needs to be let out too.
Be sure to use the slashed
marks (+) which mean to
"let out" and mark how much
on the CB seam.

4. Remember to draw a smooth
line and sew before ripping
the old line out. Be very
careful not to cut the fabric while ripping.

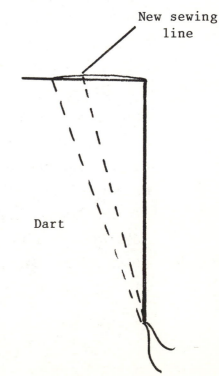

New sewing
line

Dart

5. If the waistband does
not have a CB seam, you may
have to remove it as you did
when taking the waist in,
and splice a small extension
onto the CF by the button.
If there is not a CB seam
allowance to let out, or if
the zipper is in the back,
you may have to let out the
sideseams. Darts can also
be let out if more fabric
is needed.

6. If the pants are very tight, they may be pulling in the stride also, (back of the thighs) and need to be let out.

Again, it is hard to determine how much to let out the stride because there is no way to measure this. I usually let the amount of increase in the waist and seat determine how much I let out the stride.

In general, if the pants are let out in the waist and seat 1" to 1½", I would let out the stride about 1". This is only on the back seam. If the waist and seat were let out more than 1½" and the stride looked very tight, I would let it out about 1 3/4 to 2".

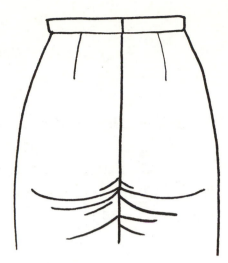

The pants are pulling in the stride.

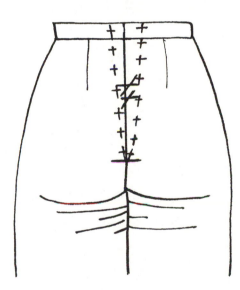

Diagonal slash lines through stride marks mean "let out this much"

If there is not enough fabric to let out in the back seam, let out the front seam too. If there isn't enough there, you could add a crotchpiece (refer to the "Crotch Adjustment" section for details on this) if matching fabric is available.

Crotch Adjustment

Taking in the Crotch

1. If the crotch needs to
be taken in, the customer
will usually complain that
she feels the pants "bubble
out" or that there is extra
fabric in the crotch area.

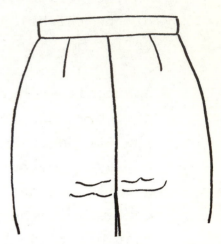

Front

This is different from
the crotch depth being too
long, which is corrected by
dropping the waistband.

Crotch depth

Extra crotch fabric usually
occurs because the crotch
curve is too long.

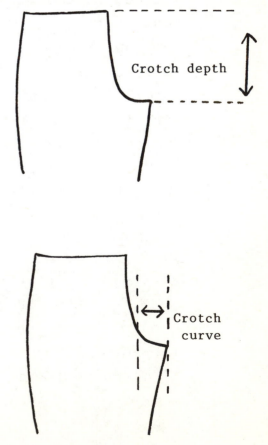

Crotch
curve

2. Fabric will need to be pinned out of the front seams only just below the crotch. If you are uncomfortable doing this or if you feel the customer will be embarrassed, make a mental estimate of the amount to be taken in.

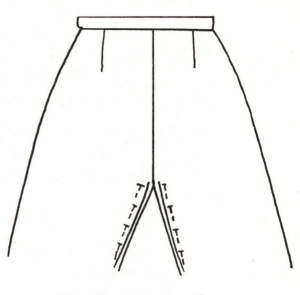

The front seam only is pinned.

Ask the customer to remove the pants so you can pin them. Then she can slip them on again to check the fit.

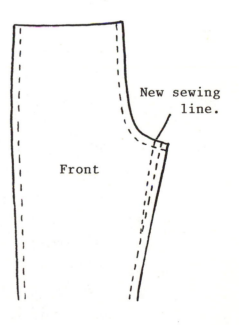

New sewing line.

Front

3. Draw your new lines and take in on the front seam only.

Letting Out the Crotch

1. When the crotch needs to be let out, the customer will almost always state that the pants feel too tight in the crotch. The pants will have pull lines coming directly from the crotch.

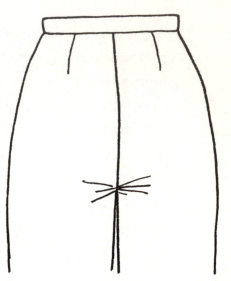

Front pull lines

2. Since it is hard to fit this problem, you will get an idea of how much to let out by asking the customer if the crotch is slightly tight or very tight.

If she replies, "Just a little tight," it probably needs to be let out ¼ to ½".

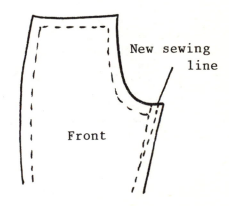

New sewing line

Front

Depending upon how much fabric there is in the seam, you may have to let out the back seam too, especially if the customer says the crotch is very tight. Let the seams out, tapering to nothing about 4" below the crotch. Sew these new seams twice since the crotch is a high stress area.

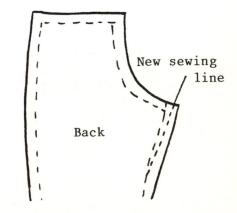

New sewing line

Back

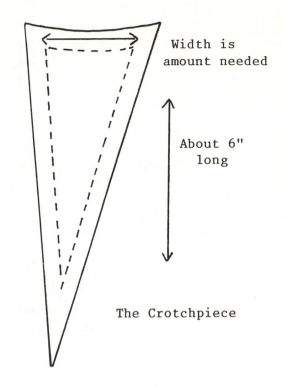

Width is
amount needed

About 6"
long

The Crotchpiece

3. If the customer has gained weight, wants extra fabric in the crotch for ease of movement (such as in sportswear), or has a worn area in the crotch, you can sometimes add a crotchpiece. The crotch-piece is a triangular piece of fabric, usually about 6" long, and as wide at the top as is needed.

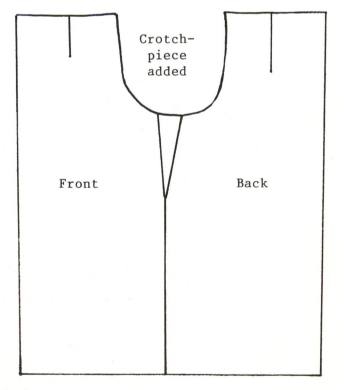

Crotch-
piece
added

Front

Back

Of course, a crotchpiece can only be added if there is matching fabric available. Sometimes a piece can be taken from the hem.

Tapering Pant Legs

This alteration is done to update out-of-style pants, or to scale down pant legs so they are more in proportion with the customer's body. Take the measurement from a pair of pants the customer likes, because it is too hard to judge the width by pinning on the body.

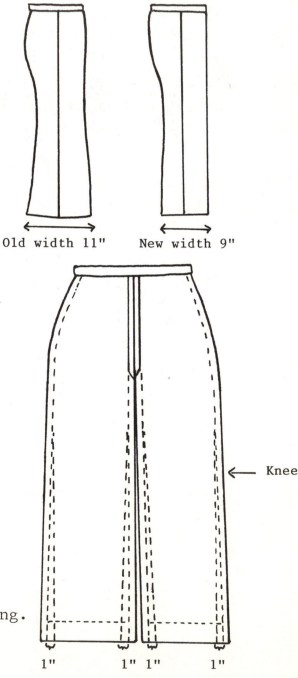

Old width 11"   New width 9"

Knee ←

1. Measure across the very bottom of the pant leg to determine the old and new widths. (Refer to "Pant Hems" section for more discussion on width.)

2. Subtract the desired width from the old width. In this case it would be 11" - 9" = 2".

3. Divide this amount by 2 and remove that much from each sideseam: 2" ÷ 2" = 1".

4. Remove the hem and draw the new sewing line, tapering to nothing about 3" above the knee.

5. Rip out the old seamline and trim the seams. Press the seams open.

6. Resew the hem and press. The pant creases remain the same.

7. If the pants are lined, repeat the process on the lining.

1"   1" 1"   1"

70

Replacing a Zipper

Before replacing a zipper, be sure to check with the customer to see if she has a preference for metal or plastic zippers.

1. Rip out the old zipper, carefully marking the sewing lines. You will also have to rip out part of the waistband that encloses the top ends of the zipper.

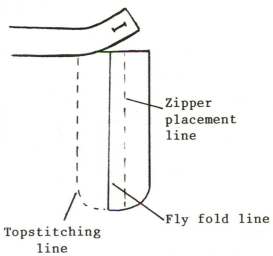

Zipper placement line

Fly fold line

Topstitching line

2. Rip out the topstitching from the fly, marking the line if it is not visible.

3. As you look at the front of the pants, stitch in the right side of the zipper from the top down. You may have to stop and move the zipper pull up or down to get it out of your way.

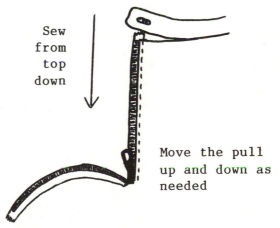

Sew from top down

Move the pull up and down as needed

4. Reapply the waistband at the top.

5. Pin or baste the zipper to the inside of the fly and sew from the top down. The zipper will be face down.

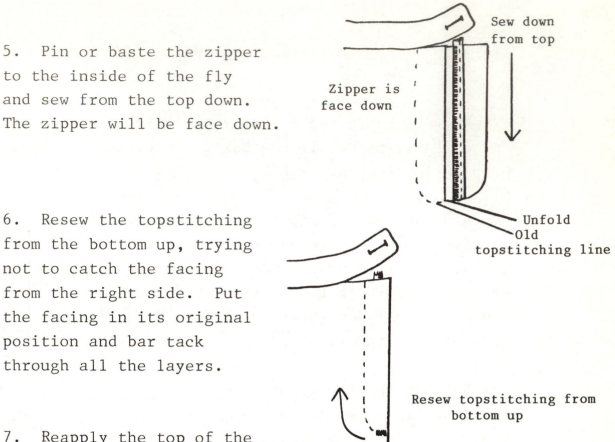

Sew down from top

Zipper is face down

Unfold
Old topstitching line

6. Resew the topstitching from the bottom up, trying not to catch the facing from the right side. Put the facing in its original position and bar tack through all the layers.

Resew topstitching from bottom up

7. Reapply the top of the waistband.

Levi zippers are much harder to replace than regular zippers. Sew slowly to reduce needle breakage. The sides in the above directions will be reversed for men's zippers. Women's flys cross right over left and men's cross left over right.

Women's fly

Men's fly

Lining or Replacing the Lining

Relining

   Occasionally you will be asked to reline pants.
Consult with the customer as to her preference for
fabrics in case you cannot find duplicate lining fabric.

1. Remove the lining and rip apart carefully, making
sure you do not stretch it out of shape. It will
probably be stretched somewhat already, so press the
pieces back in shape as well as you can.

2. Label the pieces if they are similar and make
marks or clips to show where they fit together.

3. Use the crease marks from the old lining as grain-
lines when you cut the new fabric. If the old lining
does not have 5/8" seams, you may want to cut 5/8"
seams in the new lining if that is what you're used
to sewing with.

4. Construct the lining, pressing all seams as you go.

5. Sew the new lining into the pants the same way the
old lining was inserted.

Lining Pants

You also may be asked to make a lining for pants that are unlined. Be aware that adding lining to pants will make them fit tighter. Have the customer try the pants on and if you see she already has a firm fit, mention that even thin lining adds bulk and the pants will feel slightly tighter when lined.

Some customers think adding a lining to pants will decrease wrinkling. This is somewhat true if the pants are not tight fitting. In reality, the customer's pants are probably wrinkling badly because they are too tight. (I am not speaking of fabrics that wrinkle naturally, such as linen and ramie.) I generally deal with this potentially touchy situation by explaining that the addition of lining will not be insurance against wrinkling.

Since constructing a lining can be as time consuming as making a pair of pants, I first suggest the customer buy a pant liner which is available in lingerie departments. If she insists on lining the pants, be sure to give a price quote before doing the work. Again, discuss lining fabrics to see if the customer has a preference.

1. It is easier to buy a pants pattern in the size and style of the customer's pants than to try to draw your own pattern from measuring the pants.

2. Measure the waist, hips, crotch depth, and length of the pants and adjust the pattern accordingly.

3. Cut and sew the lining.

4. You may want to have the customer try the lined pants on before you secure the lining permanently.

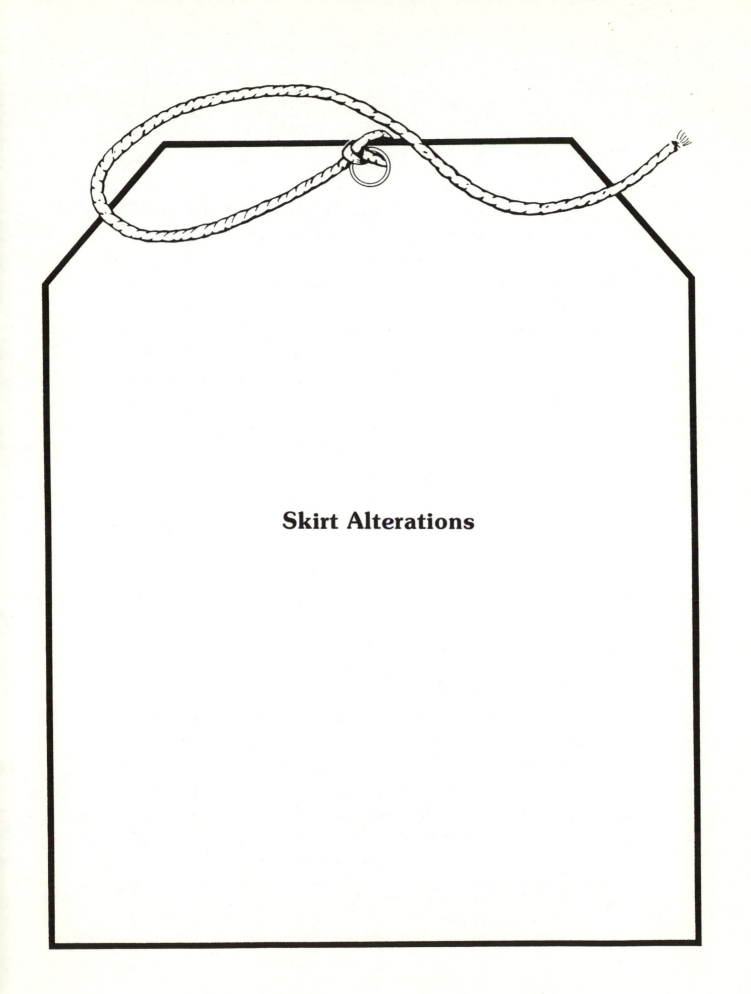

Skirt Alterations

Skirt Hems

Measuring for skirt hems is done from the floor up in order to accommodate variations in body types. Having a high hip or one leg longer than the other will cause hems to be uneven if they are measured from the waist down.

If there are any other alterations being done to the skirt, fit for them first and measure the hem last. If you are taking in or letting out the waist and/or sides, you may have to do those alterations first and then refit for the hem. This will insure accurate marking.

During the fitting, the customer must be wearing shoes the height of the ones she will be wearing with the skirt. Make sure she is standing comfortably with her weight on both feet. Tell her not to look down, but to look in the mirror if she wants to see what you are doing. Have the customer remain in one place while you go around her.

Pin the garment up in front; or if necessary, all around, so the customer can see what the length will be. You do not need to be extremely accurate doing this. After the customer has approved the length, measure how far from the floor the hem is in front with a yardstick or a hem marker.

Remove the pins and mark the hem precisely all around with chalk. When you get to the sideseams, make them about 1/8" longer than the front, and taper down to ¼" longer at the CB. If you make the skirt the same length all around, it will appear to be shorter in the back.

If the customer has a
skirt she likes the length of,
have her slip it on and measure
the distance from the floor in
the front. Then have her try
on the new skirt and mark it
all around.

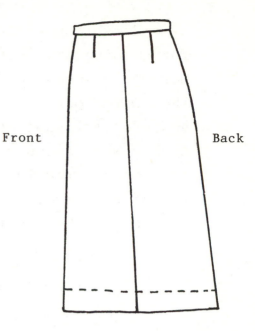

Front   Back

Make the skirt ¼" longer in
the back. Otherwise, it will
appear to "hike up" in back.

What is the proper length
for a skirt? The foremost answer is always, "The length the
customer wants." If the customer can't decide, fold the
hem up at various points on her
leg to see what she likes.
This may be different from what
you think looks good, but try
to be sensitive to what she wants.

Generally, a street length
skirt flatters the leg the most
if it stops somewhere below the
knee but above the widest part of
the calf. It may look more flattering or slimming just below the
widest part of the calf. Many
customers will be very style con-
scious and will ask for the current length. For this reason,
try to keep abreast of current
fashions.

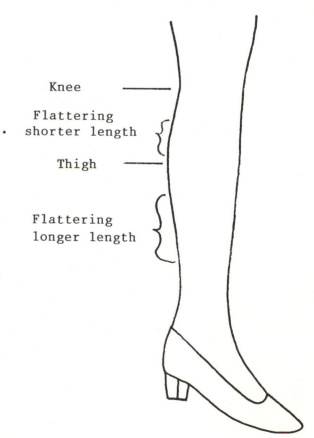

Knee ——————

Flattering
shorter length

Thigh ——————

Flattering
longer length

Hems longer than street length are usually worn for evening or special occasions. Sometimes a customer will request a "tea" length or a "waltz" length. These are located in the area just above the ankle and are very subjective according to customer preference. When a customer requests a "floor" length hem, it does not really go to the floor but just to the top of the shoe. Usually the only dresses that actually go to the floor are wedding dresses.

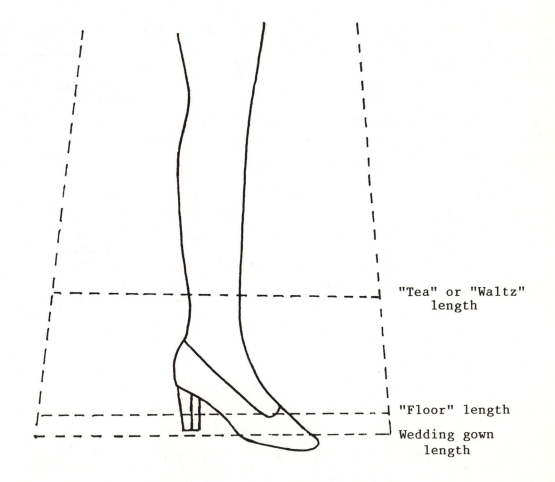

"Tea" or "Waltz"
    length

"Floor" length
Wedding gown
    length

Shortening Skirts

Straight or A-line Skirts

A straight or A-line hem should be 2 to 3". Fuller skirts usually have smaller hems. Let the size of
the old hem help dictate the size of the new hem.

1. Mark the new hemline with chalk.

2. Remove the old hem.

3. Connect the chalk marks.

4. Measure down for the new hem and cut off the excess.

5. Finish the raw edge by serging or with hem tape.
These are the two most professional finishes.

6. Press the hem up.

7. Sew the hem with a blindhemmer or use one of the
stitches listed under the "Hand Sewing" chapter. Press.

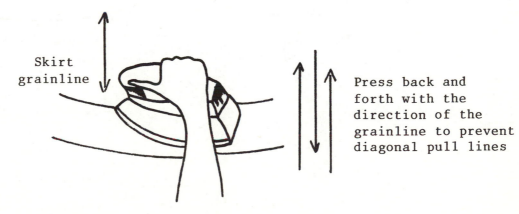

Skirt
grainline

Press back and
forth with the
direction of the
grainline to prevent
diagonal pull lines

If the skirt has a pleat, note carefully how it is sewn so you can put it back the same way. There are many variations in technique so you will have to be flexible and learn as you go.

If the skirt is shortened so much there is less than 2" of the pleat left, advise the customer that it may look better to close the pleat or to remove it if it is already closed. You probably will not be able to extend the pleat because there won't be any facing above where the pleat stops. If the skirt is lined, you might be able to extend the open pleat by using the lining as facing.

Open pleat   Closed pleat

To attach lining to the edge
of the pleat, first sew the
lining hem. The lining is
ripped from the pleat at
the bottom so you can do
this. The skirt hem is not
done yet.

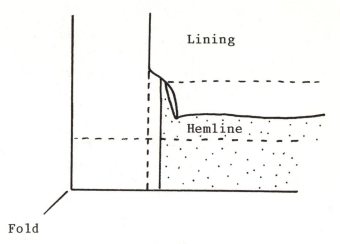

Fold the lining and skirt
right sides together and
stitch them at the bottom.

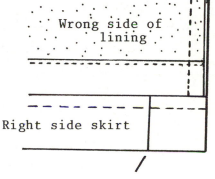

Fold the hem up on the hemline, sandwiching the lining
between the hem and the edge
of the pleat. Stitch.

When turned to the right
side, the edge will be finished.

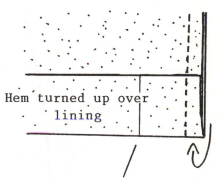

81

If the skirt is lined, shorten the lining the same amount as the skirt. Always check to see that it isn't hanging down before you sew. It is very acceptable to stitch the lining hem on the machine. It will be faster and more durable.

Full Skirt

On a full skirt, the hem may have excess fullness when turned up. If the fullness is slight, try first to ease it in with the iron. If the fullness is slight, but cannot be eased with the iron, you may be able to take in each seam from the hemline down.

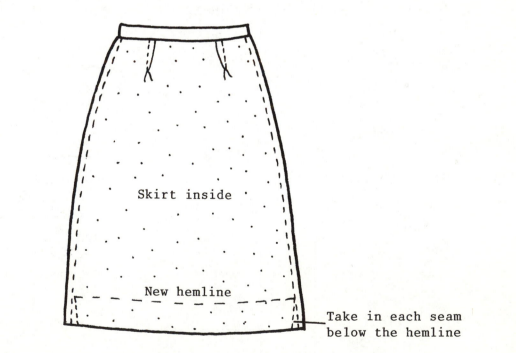

Skirt inside

New hemline

Take in each seam below the hemline

Skirt Front

If the skirt is very full, you will have to run
a basting thread and ease in the fullness. Fold the
hem up so you can see if you have eased enough and
press with the grain as discussed in straight and A-line
hems. Then apply seam tape to stabilize the eased fabric. When pressing, you may have to put a piece of
paper between the hem and the inside of the skirt so
the ease marks won't show through on the right side.
The smaller the hem, the less ease will be needed.

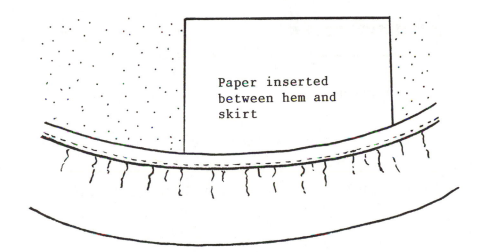

Paper inserted
between hem and
skirt

Eased hem

Topstitched Hems

If the hem is topstitched, ask the customer if she wants the same type of hem. Try to be very accurate in your marking since there won't be any fabric or very little to let out.

Study the original hem and duplicate it as closely as possible. If the hem is rolled over twice and top-stitched, you can make a less bulky seam by serging and then folding up once. Topstitch through the line of serging.

Hem inside   Hem outside

If the hem is very small and rolled, try using the machine attachment that does this stitch. It will roll the fabric under twice and stitch all in one motion.

Another alternative to the rolled hem is to serge the edge and turn it up just enough to hide the serging. Topstitch through the serging.

If the fabric does not ravel, such as with a knit, try stitching on the hemline to stabilize it. Then turn the hem up and topstitch it.

Wedding Gown with or without a Train

As mentioned before, a wedding gown usually comes all the way to the floor. Turn it up at the floor and mark it all around. Shorten it according to previous instructions in this chapter.

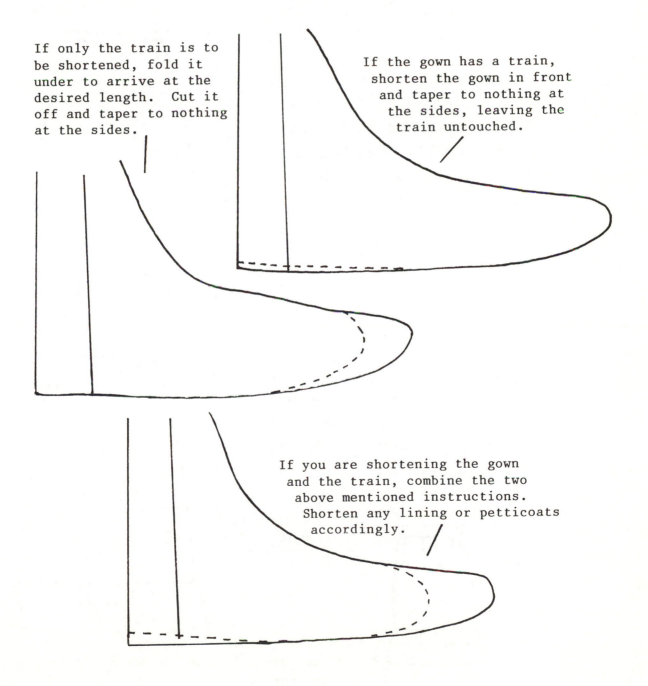

If only the train is to be shortened, fold it under to arrive at the desired length. Cut it off and taper to nothing at the sides.

If the gown has a train, shorten the gown in front and taper to nothing at the sides, leaving the train untouched.

If you are shortening the gown and the train, combine the two above mentioned instructions. Shorten any lining or petticoats accordingly.

Skirt with a Ruffle

Shortening a skirt with a ruffle will be a subjective decision. Learn to analyze the proportions of the skirt and the ruffle in order to decide where to shorten it.

1. If it needs shortening only a small amount and it is even, you may be able to just shorten the ruffle.

Shortening the ruffle only.

2. If it needs to be shortened a lot, remove some from the ruffle and some from the waist to keep the proportions in balance.

Marks on waist and ruffle.

Divide this amount by 2 and take half from the waist and half from the ruffle

3. If it needs to be shortened a medium amount or if the hem is going to be very uneven, shorten it from the waist. Mark the amount to be shortened at the bottom as usual on the CF, CB, and sideseams. Transfer this amount to the waist and shorten from there.

When shortening from the waist, you will have to move the zipper down if you are shortening more than 3/4". If the customer has large hips in proportion to her waist, it is better to move the zipper even if you are shortening less than 3/4".

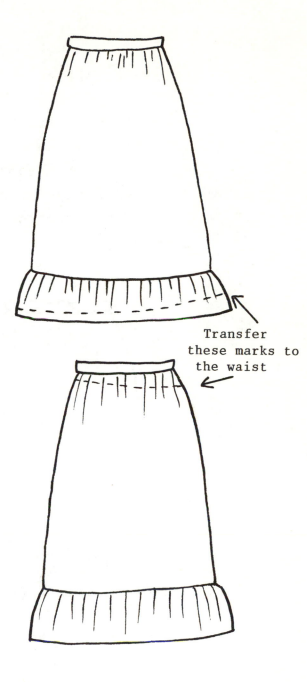

Transfer these marks to the waist

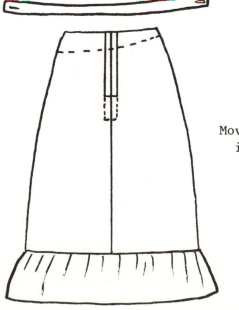

Move the zipper if necessary

Skirts with Borders

If the skirt has a border that is very obvious, you will have to decide whether shortening from the waist or hem is appropriate. The design of the border itself may dictate the answer. Be sure to receive input from the customer as to her preference before hemming.

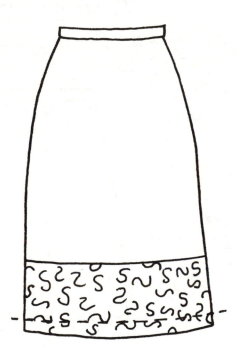

Shorten at the bottom

Shortening the border on this skirt would not be noticeable

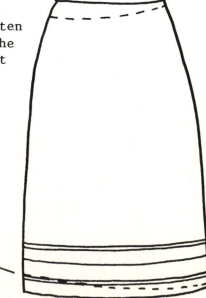

Shorten at the waist

An uneven hem would cut through the design on this border

Pleated Skirts

Pleated skirts are usually shortened from the
waist unless there are only a few pleats. This is
done in order to avoid repressing all the pleats. On
some fabrics, such as doubleknits, you would not be
able to repress the pleats even if you wanted to do so.
Mark the amount to be shortened around the bottom
and transfer the marks to the waist. You may have extra fabric to ease in at the waist. This can usually
be done by folding the pleats a little deeper as needed.
If this is not possible, remove some fullness at the
sideseams and remember to allow at least ½" extra fabric to be eased onto the waistband.

Knit Skirts

In some knit skirts, there is not a separate
waistband, but the fabric is simply folded over and
elastic is encased in it. Remove the elastic and cut
off the top of the skirt, leaving enough fabric to
fold over for the waistband. Reinsert the elastic.
Move zippers down if needed.

Marks at bottom

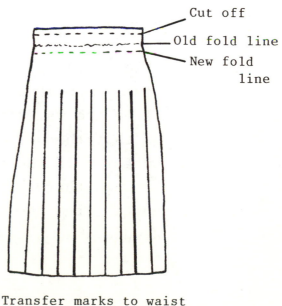

Cut off

Old fold line

New fold
line

Transfer marks to waist

89

Lace or Trimmed Hems

If there is trim or lace around the hem, as in slips, it may be easiest to remove the lace, shorten the garment, and resew the lace. Mark the hem on the bottom as usual and transfer the marks to the body of the skirt after removing the lace or trim.

Shorten this amount

Cut off

Plaid Skirts

Since most plaid skirts are also pleated, they are usually shortened from the waist too. Shortening them from the waist is necessary if there is a high hip so that the plaid lines will not be thrown off at the bottom. If the difference in side markings is slight, and there are few or no pleats, you may want to shorten from the bottom following one plaid line all around.

Lengthening Skirts

The saying, "Necessity is the mother of invention," will come into play often when lengthening skirts. This is because there usually won't be enough fabric to let out and you will need to face or find another way to lengthen the skirt.

Always use a facing that is cut on the bias, whether you buy it or make your own. This will enable you to get a smooth hem and to ease in extra fullness. Lace can also be used effectively to face hems because it has give and can be eased in.

Press out the old hem first and then apply the facing, being sure not to stretch it as you sew. You may want to pin or baste it on before the actual sewing. After it is applied, press and sew like a normal hem. (Refer to the "Lengthening Pant Hems" section for more suggestions.)

Bias hem facing

Lace hem facing

If facing the hem does not lengthen the skirt enough, you may be able to insert a horizontal stripe, lace, trim, or a ruffle.

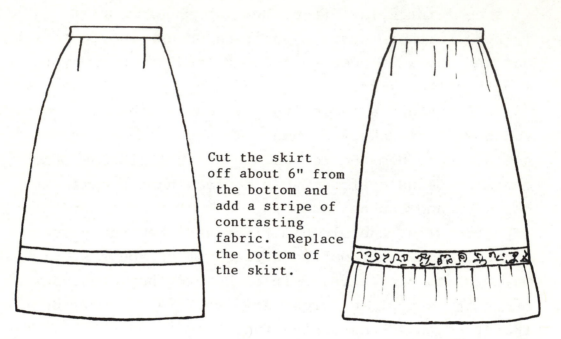

Cut the skirt off about 6" from the bottom and add a stripe of contrasting fabric. Replace the bottom of the skirt.

If the skirt has a ruffle, remove it and add a piece of lace the amount you want to lengthen it.

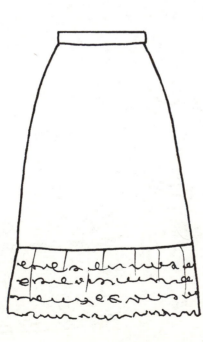

Add a piece of eyelet lace or a patterned ruffle to the bottom of a skirt that is too short.

Waist and/or Sides In or Out

Refer to these alterations on pants for instructions.

Sides in through Hem

Sometimes the skirt will need to be taken in at the sides all the way through the hem. If there are pockets in the sideseams, take the amount out of the CB seam and shorten the waistband accordingly. If there is no CB seam, ask the customer if you can make one. You will also need to cut through the CB waistband and make a seam or remove and shorten the waistband.

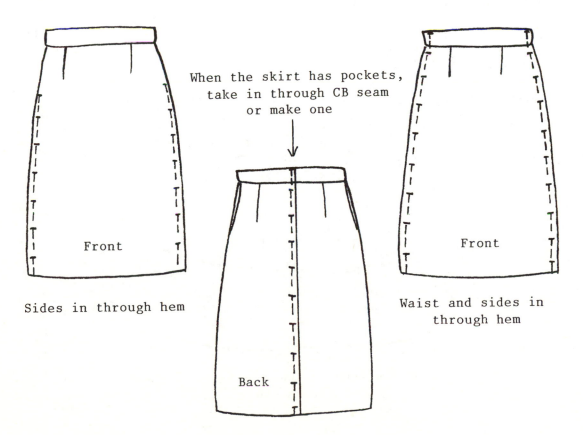

When the skirt has pockets, take in through CB seam or make one

Front

Sides in through hem

Back

Front

Waist and sides in through hem

When a seam is taken in through the hem, it will
cause the hem to pull up right at the seamline. Let
out the hem slightly at the seams that have been taken
in so that the hemline will be smooth.

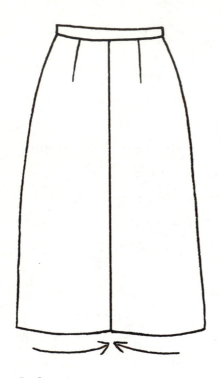

Before straightening, the
hem pulls up

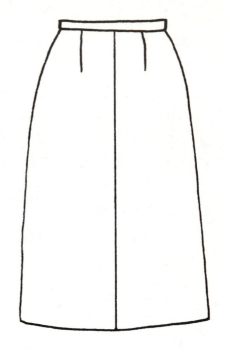

After straightening

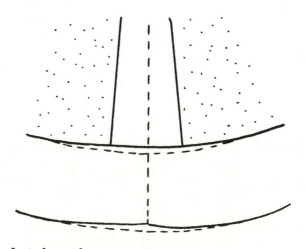

Let hem down at the seam to make the
curve smooth

If the customer wants you to take in the sides of a skirt so much that it changes from an A-line to a straight skirt, be sure the customer can still walk freely after pinning. If not, you will have to make a slit in the CB or sideseam for freedom of movement.

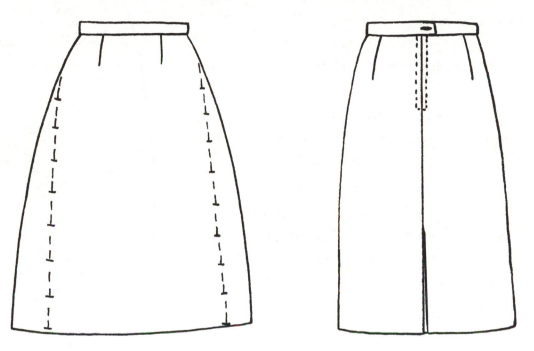

Replacing a Skirt Zipper

Refer to "Pants" chapter for directions.

Replacing Elastic in the Waist

If the customer needs the elastic replaced in the waist, always get her waist measurement so you will have a reference for how long to make the elastic. Apply the new elastic the same way the old was applied. If the elastic is not stitched to any fabric, be sure to use no-roll elastic.

Dropping the Waistband

Sometimes it may appear that the waistband on a skirt needs to be dropped because a fold of fabric will form right under the waistband.

This usually happens because the customer's waist is small in proportion to her hips or because the wide part of the customer's hips is closer to the waist than the wide hip of the skirt. This causes the skirt to sit on the hips or to ride up and produce the fold of fabric.

If the fabric is wool, or one that won't show when let out, try letting out the sideseams from just below the waist through the hip. Then the skirt can fall smoothly over the hips and you won't have to drop the waistband. If there is no fabric to let out, or if the old stitching would show, you will have to drop the waistband. (Refer to "Pants.")

Fold of fabric appears at waist.

The skirt "sits" on the hips.

Sirt Front

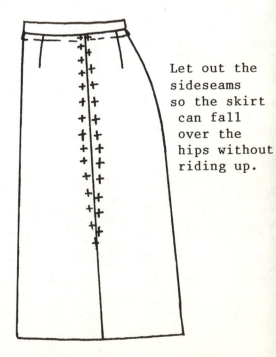

Let out the sideseams so the skirt can fall over the hips without riding up.

Skirt Side

If the waistband is dropped, there will be a lot of fabric to ease onto the waistband. Do not defeat the purpose of dropping the waistband by taking the ease out of the sideseams. This would cause the skirt to ride right back up on the hips. Because the customer's waist measurement expands quickly out to the hips, add extra front and back darts to accommodate this sharp curve. Make the darts on the outside of the original darts and about ½" shorter.

If the skirt is lined, make the same adjustments in the lining.

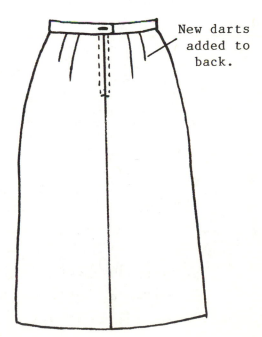

Add new darts on the outside of the original darts.

Skirt Front

New darts added to back.

97

Flat Seat

If the customer has a flat
seat, the skirt will hang
in the back.

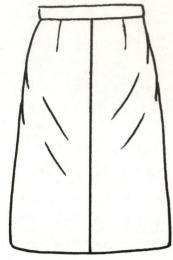

Skirt
Back

This is also easily seen
from the side.

Skirt
Side

Drop the back of the waistband
only and taper to nothing at
the sideseams.

Skirt Back

Protruding Hip Bones

When a skirt is A-line or straight, protruding hip bones will be an obvious problem. Pull lines will emanate from the hip bones.

Pull lines at hip bones

Skirt Front

The easiest way to fit for this is to rip out the darts and sideseams about 6" down from the waist. Also rip the skirt from the hip bone area.

New sewing line

Repin the sideseam, letting out the front so there will be more fabric to fit over the hip bone. Repin the dart so it points to the hip bone. You may need to make two darts rather than one.

Waistband is removed above the darts and at the sideseams. Let the front sideseam out and repin the dart or make two darts to fit over the hip bones.

Usually the customer will
know that this is the problem because she has had to
deal with it before. The
skirt will form diagonal
pull lines coming from the
high hip.

Skirt Front
with pull lines
at the high
hip.

There will also be pull
lines on the back.

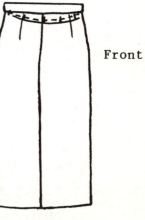

Skirt Back shows
pull lines too.

Pin and alter as for dropping the waistband (details
in "Pants" chapter).

Back   Front

Front

Slashes
show new
sewing line.

Drop the waist
at the side only.

Check to see if the hem is
shorter on the high hip
side and lengthen if nec-
essary.

You may need to
lengthen the hem
on the side of the
high hip.

Lining a Skirt

If the customer wants a skirt lined, buy a pattern that is similar to the skirt design. Compare measurements from the skirt to the pattern and adjust. (See "Lining Pants" for more details.) If the skirt has pockets, make the lining without pockets since they don't affect the lining.

When the skirt has no zipper and opens through a pocket, leave the sideseam of the lining unsewn enough to open with the pocket.

To attach the lining at the waist, undo the waistband on the inside, insert the lining, and stitch the ditch or topstitch.

To insure against pulling at the zipper, leave the lining open the length of the zipper and stitch the edges under. Let the lining hang free from the zipper.

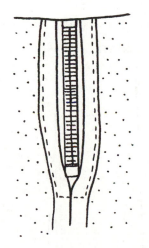

On the inside ,the lining is
left open the length of the
zipper and is turned under
and stitched. It hangs free
from the zipper.

If there is a closed pleat in the skirt, you do not make a pleat in the lining. Leave the lining seam open the length of the pleat and stitch down the seam allowance. Do not attach the lining to the pleat.

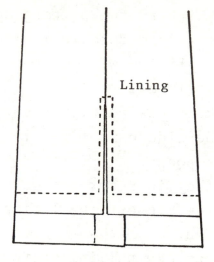

Closed pleat in the skirt with the lining left undone the length of the vent. It is topstitched and hangs free from the skirt.

Skirt Inside

If there is an open pleat, leave the lining seam open as high as the pleat and tack it to the seam allowance of the pleat. Be sure the lining is not pulling. If the pleat has topstitching around it, stitch right through the lining.

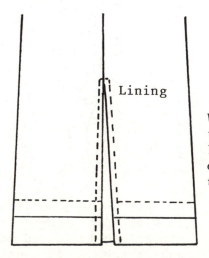

With an open vent in the skirt, turn the lining under and tack or topstitch it to the vent.

Skirt Inside

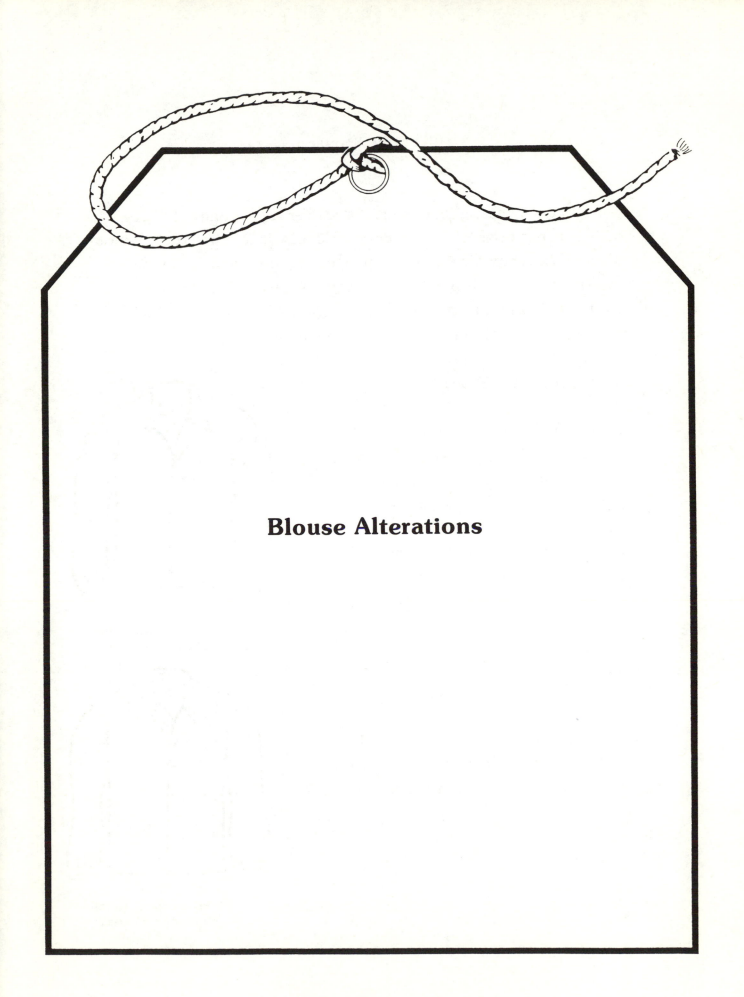

Blouse Alterations

Fitting Blouses

When fitting blouses, remember the general rule of fitting from the top down. Check the shoulder seams to see if they are in the proper place before doing sleeve hems. Also add or remove shoulder pads before fitting lower in the garment. Take in sides or add darts before shortening the blouse.

Narrowing the Shoulders

The shoulders need to be narrowed if the seams are hanging down past the shoulder bone. Sometimes the customer will complain that the blouse is too big and all that needs to be done is to narrow the shoulders.

The shoulder seams hang past the shoulders.

1. Take a tuck in the shoulder seam big enough to bring the sleeve seam up to the bone.

Tucks pinned in the shoulder seams.

2. Measure the tuck and mark
this amount on the sleeve
seam. Taper to nothing just
below the middle of the armhole.

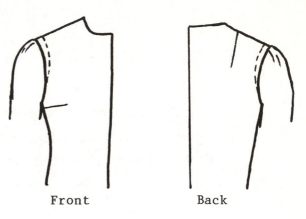

Front   Back

3. Put a pin or chalk mark
at the top of the sleeve to
show where it is attached to
the shoulder seam.

Old seam   New seamline

A pin marks
where the sleeve
attaches to the
shoulder.

4. Rip out the cap of the
sleeve and reattach on the new
sewing line. Trim and finish
the seam.

*Note: For narrowing shoulders on a princess line,
see the "Dress" chapter.

If the customer has sloping
shoulders, the blouse will
have diagonal lines running
from the armscye up toward
the neckline. In this case,
the shoulder must be dropped.

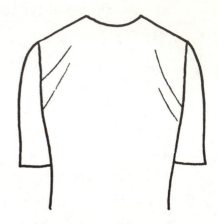

Diagonal lines point
to sloping shoulders.

You may be able to cure the
problem quickly and easily
by adding shoulder pads. If
the customer doesn't want
them, you will have to do the
alteration.

1. Pin fabric out of the
shoulder seams until the
wrinkles disappear.

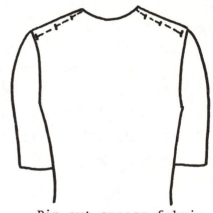

Pin out excess fabric.

2. If no more than 3/4"
total is pinned out, remove
the sleeve cap and take in
the front and back. Be sure
to mark where the sleeve
attaches to the shoulder.

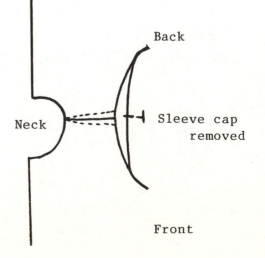

3. Rip out the old shoulder seam and press it open.

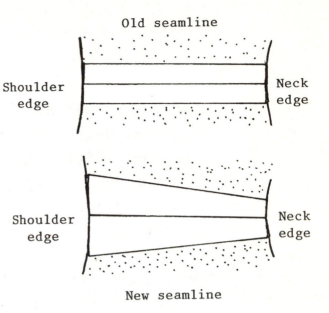

Old seamline

Shoulder edge   Neck edge

Shoulder edge   Neck edge

New seamline

4. Reattach the sleeve cap, easing in with a basting stitch if necessary.

5. Trim and finish the seam.

If the shoulder needs to be dropped more than 3/4", you must remove the entire sleeve and drop the whole armhole.

1. Mark the sleeve where it is attached at the shoulder, the front and back armscye, and the underarm.

2. Drop the armhole half of the amount you dropped the shoulder. For instance, 1" total from shoulder (½" from front and ½" from back), ÷ 2 = ½" from armhole. When you drop the armhole, curve up to nothing at the middle of the armscye.

3. Reapply the sleeve, matching the points you had marked. Trim and finish the seams.

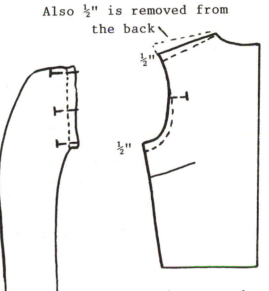

Also ½" is removed from the back

½"

½"

The sleeve is removed and the armhole is dropped. Pins mark where the sleeve attaches to the armhole.

Erect Shoulders

If the customer has very erect or square shoulders, the blouse will have pull lines going out diagonally from the shoulder.

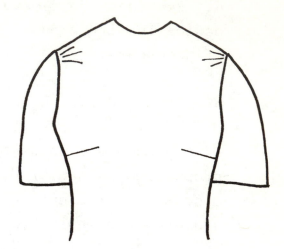

Pull lines indicate erect shoulders.

1. If the problem is not severe, you may be able to let out the shoulder seams to correct it.

2. Since it is difficult to measure how much to let out, you will usually let out all possible, tapering to nothing at the neckline.

3. Remove the sleeve cap, marking the shoulder point.

4. Let out the seam and press open.

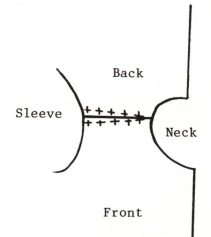

Remove the sleeve cap and let out the shoulder seams.

5. If the sleeve seems too small for the armhole, rip more of the sleeve cap out and reapply to get more ease.

If the garment has shoulder pads, you may be able to correct the problem by removing them and leaving the seam as is.

Darts

Darts may be added to the blouse in the front so the bust area will fit better. They may also be added in the back to take out some fullness.

Back Darts

1. Picture three imaginary lines down the back of the blouse, dividing it into four equal parts. One line goes through the CB and the other two lines divide the sides of the back equally.

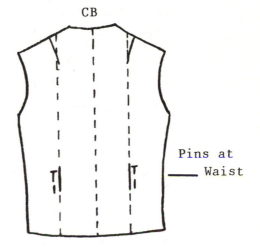

Bodice Back

2. Determine where the waist is and take two folds of fabric on the side back lines. These will be the widest points of the darts.

3. Pin up to nothing at the bottom of the shoulder blades and down to nothing about 2" from the blouse bottom (or pin all the way through the hem if needed).

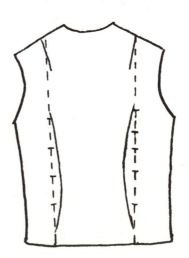

4. Transfer the marks to the inside, connect them with chalk, and sew. Press toward CB.

Darts pinned in back

109

Bust Darts

If the blouse has no bust darts and the customer is full busted (usually bigger than a "B" cup), pull lines will form naturally from the sideseams up to the bust point.

1. Put crossed pins in the blouse to designate the bust points. Be careful not to pin through the customer's undergarments.

2. Pin out a horizontal fold from the sideseam ending about 1" from the bust point. Make the fold as parallel to the waist as possible. The blouse back will be puckered where the fold is.

3. Rip open the sideseam and sew in the dart. Press the dart down.

4. The back will now be longer than the front so you will have to shorten it. Resew the sideseam and press.

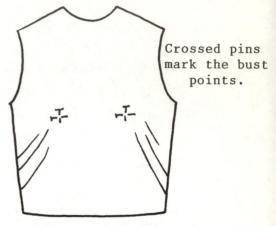

Crossed pins mark the bust points.

Diagonal lines form in the absence of darts.

Pin a dart from the sideseam to about 1" from the bust Point.

Rip the sideseam and sew the new dart.

Shorten the back to match the front.

If the front must be lengthened to match the back, see tips for facing the front in the "Short Waisted" section of the Dress Chapt.

110

Taking in the Sideseams

    If the customer wants the sides taken in, always check to see if the seams are flat felled (double top-stitched) because this will add a lot of time onto the length of the alteration. If the seams are flat felled, check first to see if back darts will remove enough fullness. If not, be sure to give a price quote which reflects the extra time that will be needed to do the alteration.

1. Pin the sides as needed.

2. If you are extending the alteration into the armhole, taper it to nothing as soon as possible.

These sideseams are pinned through the armhole.

If the seams are flat felled, remove all the stitching first and then sew the new seam.

3. Transfer markings to the inside and sew the new seam.

New sewing line on the inside.

4. Trim and finish the seams.

Gussets

If the blouse feels too tight in the armholes and you can match the fabric, you may be able to add gussets for more ease of movement. They are diamond-shaped pieces of fabric (similar to crotchpieces in pants), that are inserted in the underarms and side-seams.

The best way to fit for this is to rip open the underarm seam and measure the width of the gusset that will be needed.

Use this measurement for the widest part of the gusset. Taper to nothing about 4" each side of the measurement and add seam allowance. The gusset can be one piece or two. Cut the grainline right down the middle.

If you have cut the gusset in two parts, first sew the center seam and then apply one side at a time to the blouse.

For extra reinforcement, you can topstitch close to the seam on the outside.

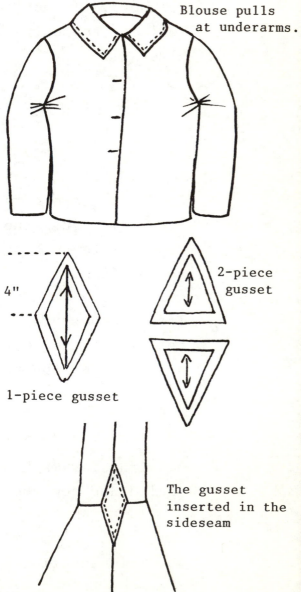

Blouse pulls at underarms.

4"

1-piece gusset

2-piece gusset

The gusset inserted in the sideseam

Shortening the Sleeves

1. Pin a fold of fabric around the sleeve above the placket.

2. Measure the amount of fold. Remove the pins and transfer the marks to the bottom of the sleeve.

3. Remove the cuff, pinning pleats above the alteration line if there are any.

4. If the sleeves are shortened more than 1", remove the placket and move it up. Do one side at a time so you can have the other side for a guide.

5. Trim fabric at the bottom to 5/8" from the new seamline.

6. Reapply the cuff on the new sewing line and top-stitch if needed.

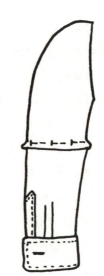

Pin out the fullness above the placket.

Transfer the marks to the bottom.

Remove the cuff and move the placket up if necessary.

Shortening Sleeves from the Top

If there is a special finish on the bottom of the sleeves, such as a border or scalloped edge, it may be necessary to shorten the sleeves from the top.

To fit, pin on the bottom as usual to determine the amount to be shortened.

Make some marks on the garment and sleeves on the fronts, backs, shoulders, and underarms. These marks will be your guides for reattaching the sleeves.

Rip the sleeves from the garment- do one at a time so you can have one for reference. Rip the sleeve seam open far enough so you can lay the cap and upper sleeve flat.

Using tissue paper, trace the top half of the sleeve. Put the connecting marks on it.

Then put the paper pattern over the sleeve and slide it down the amount to be shortened.

Cut the sleeve off, being sure to put the markings on the new seam. Resew the underarm seam and reattach the sleeve.

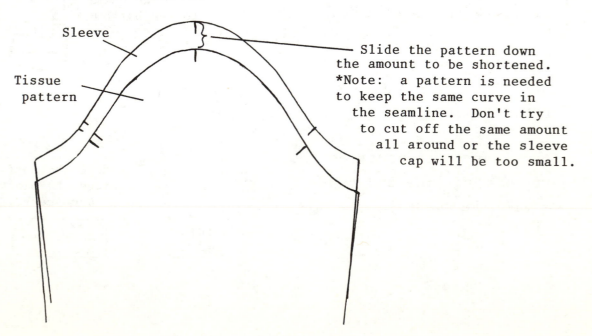

Sleeve

Tissue pattern

Slide the pattern down the amount to be shortened.
*Note: a pattern is needed to keep the same curve in the seamline. Don't try to cut off the same amount all around or the sleeve cap will be too small.

Blouse Hem

Straight Bottom

For a blouse with a straight bottom, measure the amount to be shortened and redo the hem, duplicating the original hem as closely as possible.

If it is a narrow rolled hem, try to make use of the machine attachment that does this. Another good topstitched hem with less bulk is done by serging the bottom, and then folding up the desired amount. Topstitch through the serging.

When shortening any blouse, take into consideration the position of the bottom button and buttonhole. The blouse may have to be slightly longer or shorter if the buttonhole falls right on the desired hemline.

Curved Bottom

A curved bottom is done just like a straight bottomed hem with one exception. If there is a very large curve up to the sides, don't shorten the sides as much as the front and back, or they may come above the waist.

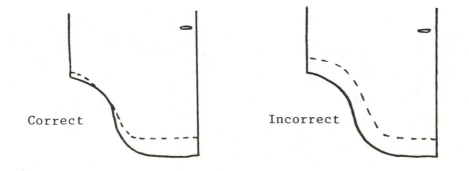

Correct   Incorrect

Narrowing the Collar

More appropriate terms for narrowing the collar might be restyling or reshaping because it is done in order to update the lines.

To determine the new collar lines, copy a collar the customer likes, or pin the collar under to obtain the desired shape. This is done in the area of the collar points only. The back of the collar is not narrowed, nor is the length of the collar shortened at the neckline.

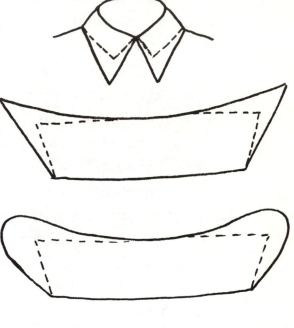

1. Remove the collar and rip out the topstitching if there is any.

Dotted lines show new collar lines.

2. Turn the collar inside out and transfer the markings to the inside. It may help to press the seams and collar flat before you sew.

Turn the collar inside out and press before sewing.

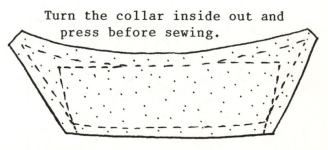

116

Diagonal stitch

3. When sewing the new lines, stitch from the CB out and down. Turn the collar and stitch from the CB out and down the other way. This will help keep the collar symmetrical.

Sew from CB out

4. At the corners, stop a stitch short of the point, take a diagonal stitch over the point, and continue stitching. This will make the point squarer when it is right side out.

Trim the seams diagonally over the corners.

5. Trim the seams closely. Trim diagonally over the points.

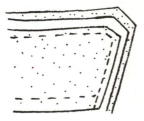

If the collar points are curved, trim closely with a pinking shears. This will make a very smooth curve when turned right side out.

6. After trimming, turn the collar right side out and press. Replace the topstitching, stretching the edges of the collar slightly as you go. To keep the points of the collar from being "eaten" by the machine, thread a needle and take a stitch through the point. Pull on the thread when you sew around the point.

Trim curved corners with a pinking shears.

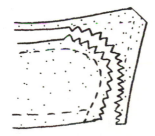

7. Resew the collar onto the blouse.

Use a needle and thread to keep the corners from being "eaten" when topstitched.

Neckline Zipper in a Sweater or Knit Top

Replacing a Zipper

1. Rip the old zipper from the garment very carefully. The seam will probably be very small and the knit could run if stretched. Note how the zipper was applied.

2. As you look at the garment, sew the right side
of the zipper first.

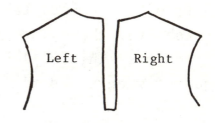

Garment back

Go to the inside and put the
right side of the opening on
the right side of the zipper.

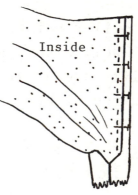

Inside

Right side of
zipper is face
up.

You may have to
move the zipper
pull up or down
as you sew.

If the garment is a turtleneck, the zipper may extend
up to the fold of the turtleneck.

In this case, stitch the zipper from the fold down. Then
turn the turtleneck at the
fold, right sides together,
over the zipper and stitch.

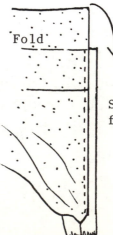

Fold

Stitch first,
fold, restitch.

When unfolded, the zipper
tape in the turtleneck will
be encased.

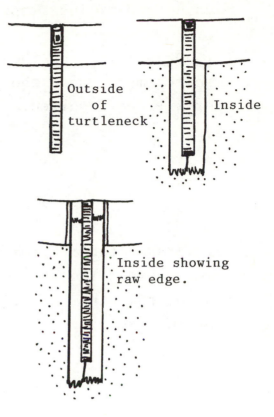

Outside
of
turtleneck   Inside

Inside showing
raw edge.

Usually there is just a raw
edge all the way to the top.

3. Repeat the same process
on the left side.

4. Go to the bottom and
stitch over the little triangle. Check on the right
side to see that you haven't
pulled it under too far.

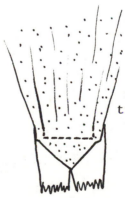

Stitch only
through the
zipper and
triangle, not
the body of
the garment.

Adding a Neckline Zipper

1. Draw a line on the garment to mark where the zipper will be inserted.

**Bodice Back
with new zipper
line.**

2. Staystitch ¼" from the
line, across the bottom,
and up the other side. Try
not to stretch the garment.

**Staystitch ¼" from the
new zipper line.**

3. Slash on the center line
down to ¼" from the bottom.
Slash diagonally to the corners.

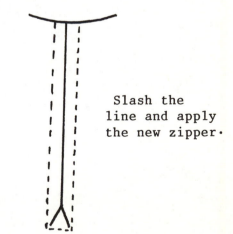

**Slash the
line and apply
the new zipper.**

4. Insert the zipper as
described above.

120

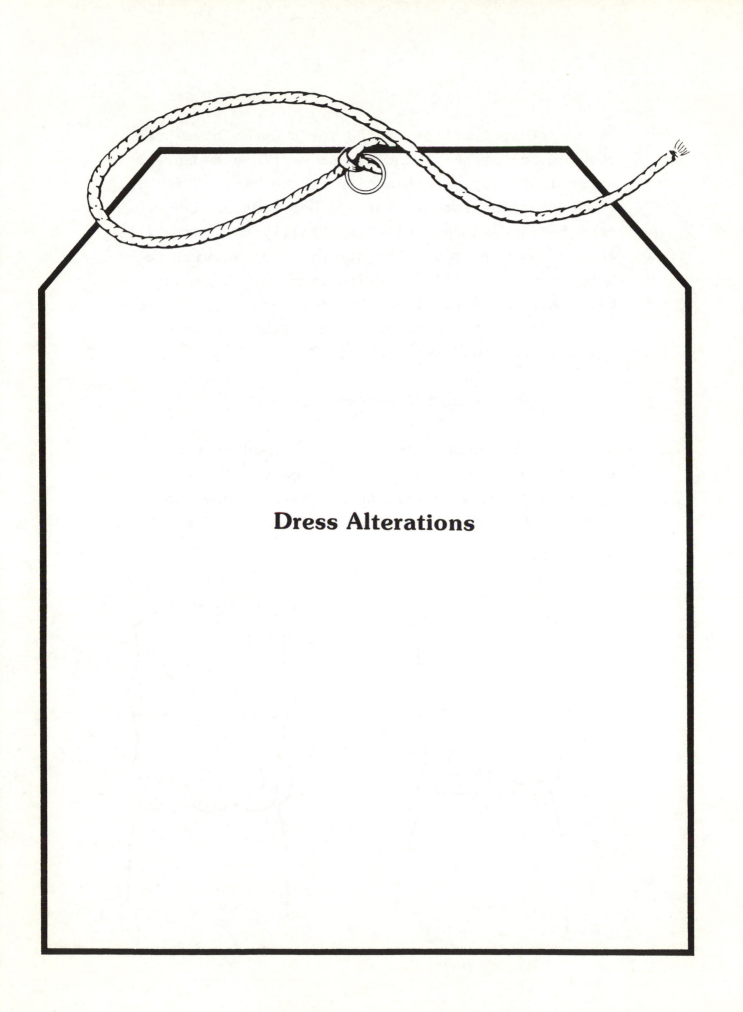

Dress Alterations

Most alterations needed for dresses have been covered in the skirt and blouse sections because a dress is merely a combination of the two. Refer to those sections for alterations not mentioned here.

Because women's clothing usually has very little seam allowance, most alterations that we will be concerned with will be taking in rather than letting out. All the directions can be reversed in the following way if the garment is too tight: just substitute "let out" for "take in."

Long Waisted and Blouson

A very common alteration performed on dresses is to shorten the bodice. This is needed when the dress is too long waisted for the customer or when there is too much fabric at the waist as a result of the blouson style.

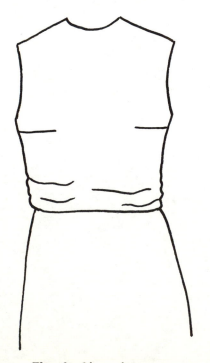

The bodice is too
long waisted

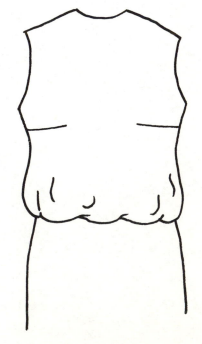

Too much Blouson

122

For long waisted, pin
a fold of fabric out around
the bodice just above the
waist. Be sure to leave a
little extra for ease of movement.

A fold of
extra fabric is
pinned out of the
long waisted bodice

Long waisted bodice

If the dress is blouson,
pin it in the same way. Be
careful not to over fit and
remove all the blouson.

For blouson, pin out
fabric above the waist.

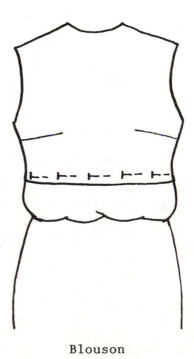

Blouson

1. Mark the bodice and skirt at CF, CB, sideseams, and any other significant connecting points.

2. Rip the bodice from the skirt. If there is a zipper in the back, you'll have to remove it completely from the skirt. Rip the zipper high enough in the bodice to be out of the alteration area.

3. Measure the amount of fabric you folded out and transfer the marks to the bottom of the bodice.

4. Cut off the excess fabric and resew the bodice to the skirt. Finish the seam and press.

5. Resew the zipper, cutting the excess off at the bottom. Stitch over the bottom several times to keep the zipper from pulling apart.

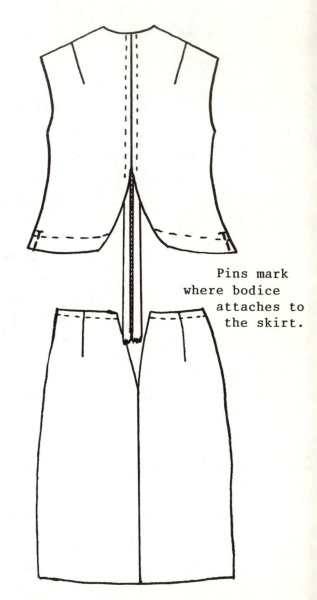

Pins mark where bodice attaches to the skirt.

Remove the bodice and zipper and shorten the bodice.

When the dress is short
waisted, there is rarely
enough if any fabric to
let out.

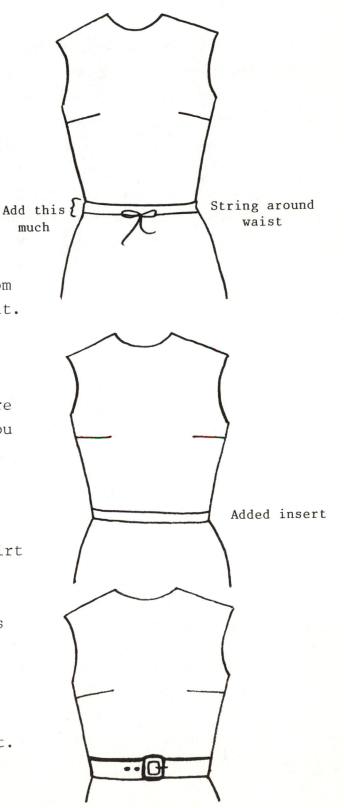

Add this { much String around waist

If the dress is fitted,
you may be able to add a
band of fabric to the bottom
of the bodice to lengthen it.

Tie a string around the
real waist to find out where
it is. This will enable you
to measure how much to add.

Added insert

Rip the bodice from the skirt
and insert the additional
fabric. You will have to
redo the zipper if there is
one in the back seam.

Hide the splice with a belt.

The purpose of a dart is to create a pooch of fullness that allows the garment to fit over a body curve. If the dart ends too soon, the pooch falls short of its intended position and does not allow fullness for the largest part of the curve. If the dart extends beyond the largest part of the curve, the purpose of creating the pooch is defeated and the garment will feel too tight. Improperly fitted darts can ruin the fit and look of the whole dress.

Bust darts should point directly to the apex or point of the bust, and should stop about 3/4 to 1" before it.

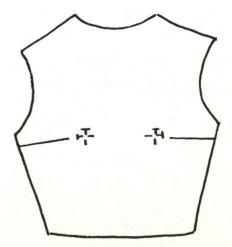

1. Put two crossed pins at the bust points to use as fitting guides. No woman is perfectly symmetrical, so the pins may not be level.

This is all the fitting you
need to do for dart position.

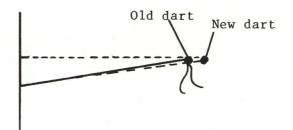

2. Go to the inside and
mark the bust point. Then
mark where the point of
the dart should be. If
the new dart point is not
more than ½" from the old
dart point, simply extend
or shorten the dart.

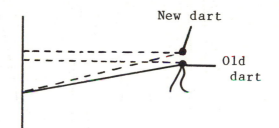

If the new dart point is
more than ½" from the old
dart point, you must move
the whole dart. This cannot be done if the stitching
shows when the old dart is
ripped out.

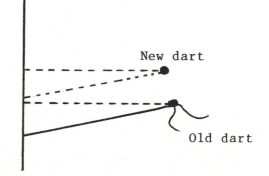

"The fit of the bodice is in direct
proportion to your age: for every
5 years over 20, lower the bust dart
1 inch!"

When the customer has sway
back, the dress will form
horizontal folds of fabric
below the back waist.

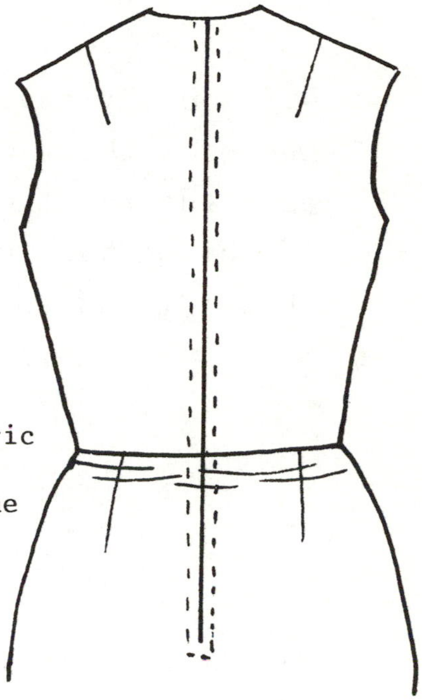

**Folds of fabric
form at the
back below the
waist.**

1. Pin out the excess fabric. Taper to nothing as
close to the sideseams as
possible.

2. Rip the waist seam
open as far as is needed.
Be sure to mark points
where the bodice and skirt
are connected. Also rip
the zipper out of the skirt
back.

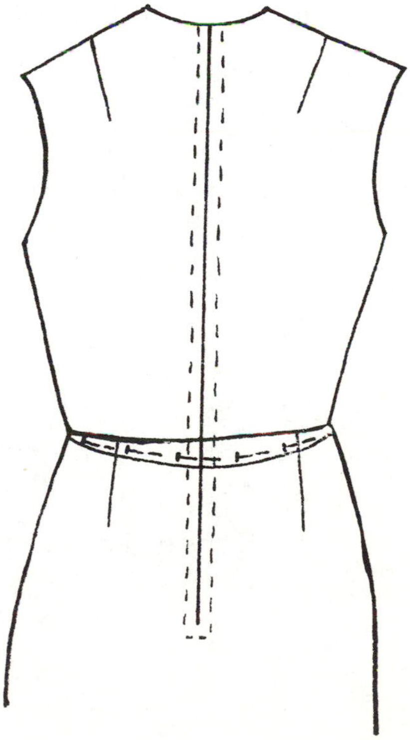

**Pin out the
excess.**

3. Transfer markings to the
inside and sew on the new
seamline.

4. You may have to take in
the back skirt darts to help
ease the skirt onto the bodice.
If this makes the dart bigger
than 1", add another dart.

5. If you are lowering the
seam more than 3/4", you
must open the CB seam and
extend the zipper too.

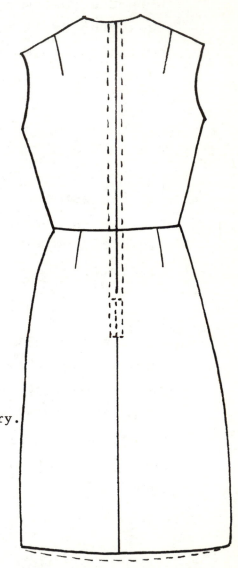

Extend the
zipper into the
seam if necessary.

6. Check the back hem of
the skirt to see if it is
pulling up. You may have to
lengthen it slightly.

Check to see if the hem needs
to be lengthened.

Taking in the Back

Sometimes the bodice front
will fit well but the bodice
back will be too large.
fabric will hang loosely on
the back forming vertical
curves.

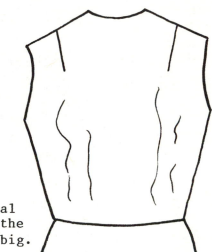

**Loose vertical
curves mean the
back is too big.**

1. Pin on the back only as
needed. Depending on how
high the looseness is, pin
the back sideseams or the
back sideseams and the lower
back armhole.

**Pin the excess out
of the back only.**

Be sure not to over fit in
this area. Pin enough to
correct the problem, but
not enough to hinder movement.

**You may only need
to pin out full-
ness from the
back sideseams.**

2. Transfer the markings
to the inside.

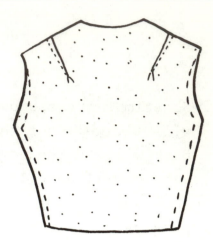

3. Rip the sideseams and
lower the armhole if needed.

4. Take in as marked and
resew the seams.

5. If you took in the lower
armhole, trim the seam and
finish.

*Note: if the back is too
tight it will have pull marks.
If there is enough fabric,
let out where we took in
above. If not, try adding
gussets (directions in "Blouse"
chapter).

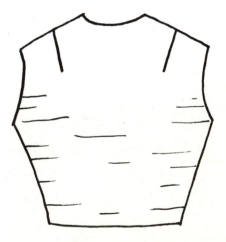

Stooped Back or Dowager's Hump

Neither one of these terms is flattering and it is unfortunate that they have come into common usage when describing this figure problem. Try using the words "rounded back" or "high rounded back" when dealing with the customer.

Obvious pull lines radiate out from the "hump".

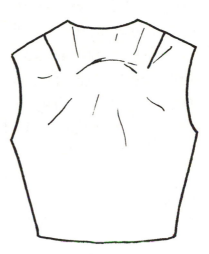

Bodice Back

From the side, the back may pull away from the neck.

The back may pull away from the neck above the hump.

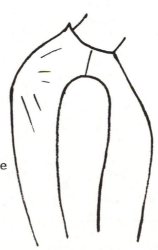

Of course, the best time to adjust for this problem would be before the garment is constructed. At that time, extra fabric can be added to accommodate the hump.

As an alterationist, about all you can do is to add darts at the neckline. This will help smooth out the back. The new darts may extend longer than normal darts.

Since the back is the obvious problem, usually this is all that is done.

New darts

Bodice Back

The front of the garment however, will probably be affected too. This is because the customer's posture is tilted forward. Wrinkles of extra fabric may form across the chest and above the waist. Again, the perfect way to remedy this is in pattern drafting. If the customer vehement and wants to do anything possible, you can try the following alterations.

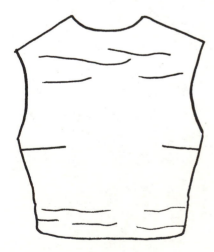

The front may have folds of extra fabric at the chest and above the waist.

To correct the chest wrinkles,
drop the neckline and take in
the front shoulder seam, tapering to nothing at the armhole.

**Pin out the
fullness.**

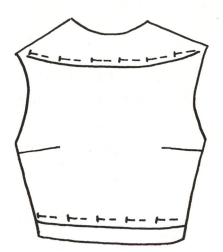

To remove the waist wrinkles,
raise the waist.

**Dotted lines show
the new sewing lines.**

Lastly, check the eveness of
the hemline. It may be pulling
up in the back and drooping in
the front.

Back   Front

     The degree of deformity will be different with
each customer and you will be wise if you do not guar-
antee a perfect fit. Usually the customer will be
very grateful for any adjustment that helps. This is
a very good example of where a custom made garment
would be advisable in the future. It may even be more
economical in the long run due to the extensive alterations needed for a ready made garment.

High Hip and Low Shoulder

This condition is usually caused because the customer has scoliosis, ordinarily know as curvature of the spine. It is a fairly common problem, but I have learned from experience not to make any medical diagnoses for customers who may be unaware of the cause. With scoliosis, the spine curves in the shape of an "S". This results in a low shoulder in the bodice and a high hip in the skirt. They will both be on the same side.

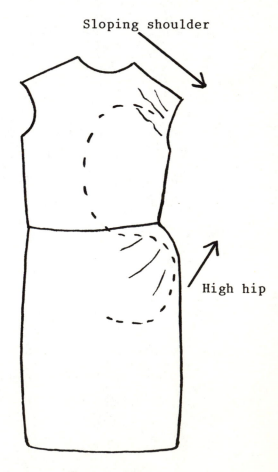

Sloping shoulder

High hip

Regardless of the cause, always refer to the alteration by what it is: high hip and low shoulder (or sloping shoulder).

When both shoulders are low or sloping, it is customary to pin the shoulder seams. In this case, it would look very unsymmetrical to drop one shoulder and not the other. The easiest way to correct the problem is to add a shoulder pad to the low side. However, if the customer objects to this, you will have to alter. Refer to the "Blouse" chapter for sloping shoulders.

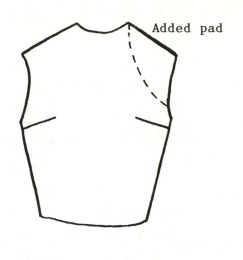

Added pad

Dropping the shoulder

For the skirt, alter as for a high hip. Details are in the "Skirt" chapter.

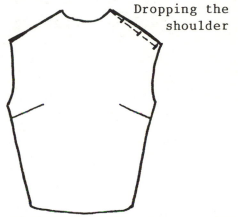

Pin out fabric above the high hip.

This is another figure problem which would best be fitted with a custom made garment.

Lengthen the skirt on the side of the high hip if needed.

Sleeves Too Tight

When the sleeves are too
tight, there will be pull
lines going horizontally
across the sleeve. Also,
the customer will undoubt-
edly say that the sleeves
feel too tight.

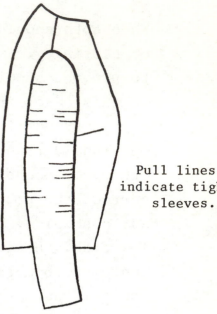

Pull lines
indicate tight
sleeves.

Check the sleeve seams to
see if there is enough to
let out. If not, you could
possibly add a gusset.
(Details in "Blouse" chapter.)
The gusset will be long and
thin.

Sleeve with
gusset

If you add a gusset in the
sleeve and not in the bodice,
you will have to drop the
underarm seam so the enlarged
sleeve will fit onto it.

Dropping the
underarm seam

Sleeves Too Loose

When the garment is fitted,
and the sleeves are too loose,
vertical curves will form on
them.

**Vertical curves
indicate loose
sleeves.**

Pin out the excess on the
underarm seam, being careful not to over fit.

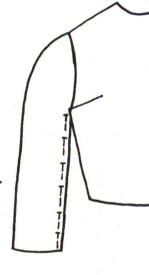

**Pin out
the excess.**

Transfer the markings to
the inside and take in as
needed.

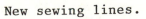

New sewing lines.

Incorrect Sleeve Pitch

Incorrect sleeve pitch will cause diagonal lines in the cap of the sleeve.

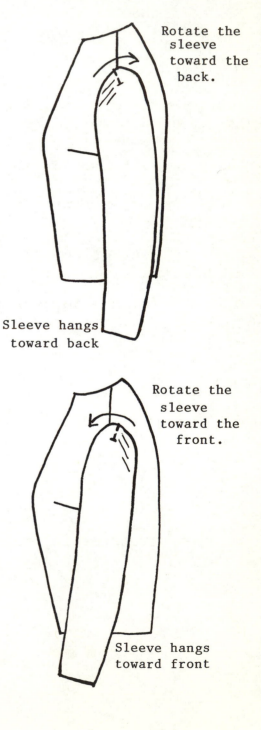

Rotate the sleeve toward the back.

Sleeve hangs toward back

If the lines are on the front, the sleeve needs to be rotated toward the back.

In each case, put a pin in the sleeve cap, indicating the new shoulder dot.

Rotate the sleeve toward the front.

If the lines are on the back, the sleeve needs to be rotated toward the front.

Sleeve hangs toward front

Because this is hard to fit, you may want to remove the sleeve and actually "hang" or "set" it on
the customer by pinning it in place. The underarm
seams or dots may not match after sleeve rotation.
An average amount to rotate the sleeve is ½" in blouses,
and 1" in jackets (remember to alter lining too). Because of the time needed to remove the sleeve, it is
lucky that this is a fairly uncommon alteration. If
the rotation needed is slight, you may only have to remove the cap of the sleeve.

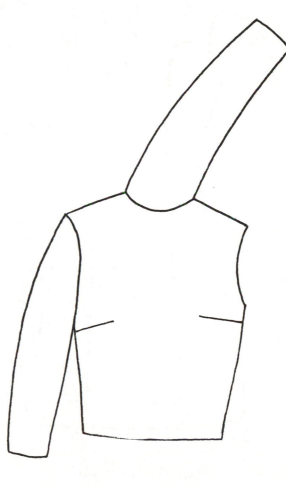

"I wondered why the notches
didn't match!"

Princess Lines

Dresses with princess lines are easier to fit
than dresses with a waist seam because there are so
many more seams to use when altering.

True Princess Line   Modified Princess Line

In general, fit on the sideseams first. If you need
to take in or let out more
than the sideseams allow,
distribute the amount over
all the seams.

"Let out"
marks

Remember to draw smooth alteration lines which go to
nothing gradually.

Shoulders
pinned for
narrowing

If the princess line is on
the front and back of the
dress, you can narrow the
shoulders there rather than
removing the sleeves.

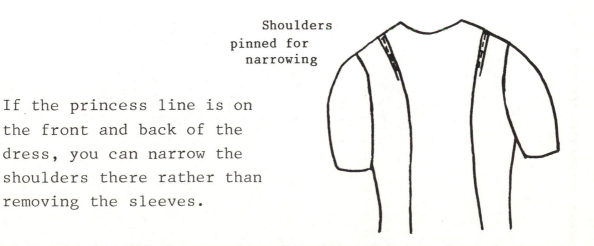

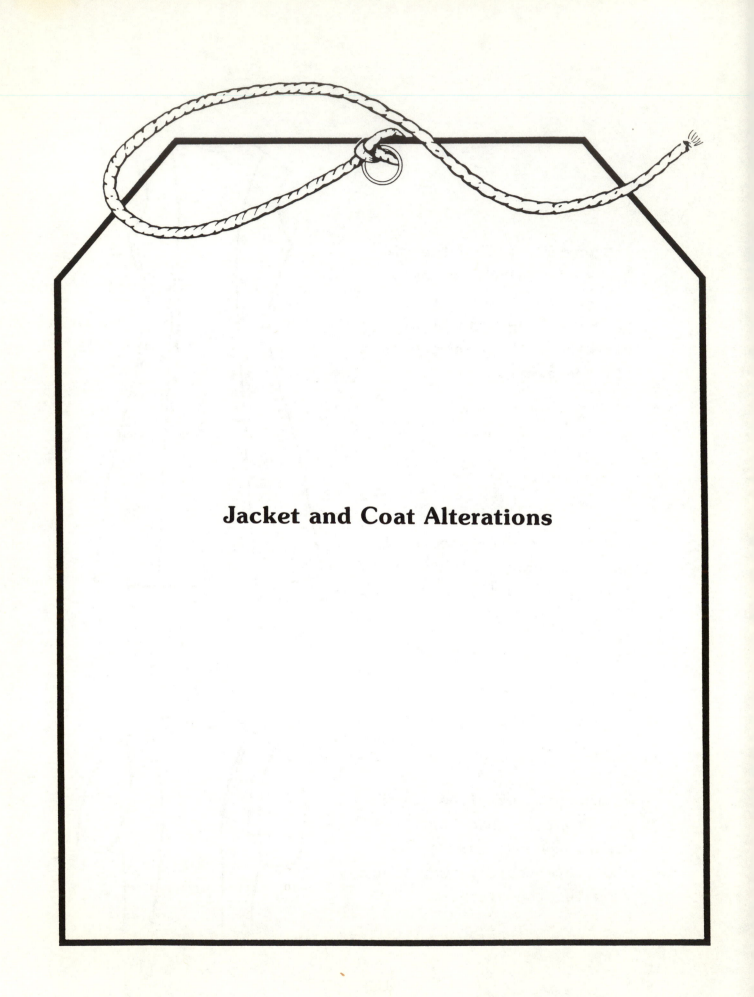

Jacket and Coat Alterations

Sleeves

Shortening or lengthening sleeves will probably be some of the most common alterations for jackets and coats. What is the proper length for a woman's jacket or coat sleeve? Remembering that the customer's preference always takes precedence over any rule, here are the guidelines:

With arms at her sides, have the customer bend her hands upward. The sleeve comes to the bend of the wrist.

A coat sleeve should be ½ to 1" longer than a jacket sleeve.

When you have determined the desired length of the sleeve, fold it under and mark it with chalk, or measure the amount to be lengthened. Whenever marking a sleeve hem, always make it a little longer than measured (whether lengthening or shortening), because the sleeve will "draw up" after it is worn.

Shortening Sleeves without Vents

With all sleeves, do one and use the other as a guide.

1. Draw a continuous chalk mark around the sleeve on the new hem-line. Measure the amount to be shortened and make a record of it. This can be done easily with an adjustable seam gauge.

A seam gauge can easily record the amount to be shortened.

2. Remove the buttons if there are any.

3. Turn the sleeve inside out and look for a seam in the lining that has been topstitched together. Rip it open. If there isn't evidence of one, rip open about 5" of any sleeve seam in the elbow area.

4. Pull the cuff inside out through the hole.

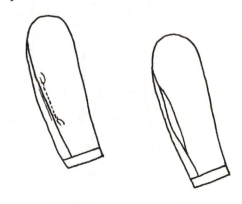

5. Rip out any threads that are tacking the hem up.

6. Find the sewing line where the lining is attached to the bottom of the sleeve. Measure up from the seam the amount to be shortened. Sew on that line, as if you are going around a tube. If you are shortening more than ½", you must move the interfacing up.

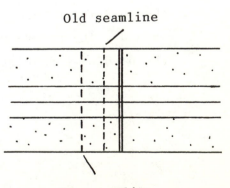

Old seamline

New seamline

146

7. Trim excess fabric if there is more than 2".

8. Turn the sleeve right side out. The lining will automatically pull the hem up. Press on the new hemline, turning all seam allowances upward. Tack the hem in place at the seamlines.

9. Topstitch the seam that you opened in the lining after you are sure the hem is sewn correctly.

10. Resew the buttons. If you resew them on the machine, use extreme caution. It is easy to break one and you will have a very hard time matching buttons on ready-mades. Also, be sure to tie off the threads because they will unravel quickly if you don't.

11. Give the hem a final press. Never press a lengthwise crease in the sleeve. To avoid this, fold a towel so it fits snugly in the hem and press with the towel in place. There are special pressing mits made for this purpose, but they are only one size. By using a towel, you can fold it to any size. Insert the towel into the sleeve in the same position that the customer's arm would be in.

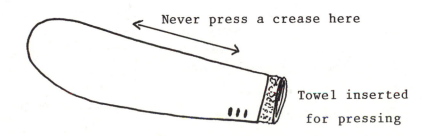

Never press a crease here

Towel inserted
for pressing

Shortening Sleeves with Vents

1. When the sleeves have vents, you will usually have to shorten them by hand. Mark the new hemline all around.

2. Remove the buttons.

3. Rip the lining from the hem and rip the hem. Rip the interfacing and move it up.

4. If there is a mitered corner, following are the steps for mitering:

a. On the inside, draw the new hemline.

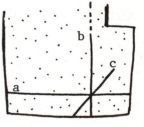

b. Draw a chalk line on the fold line of the vent.

c. Draw a 45° diagonal line through the intersection of lines a and b.

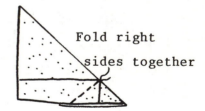

Fold right sides together

d. Fold the diagonal line together and stitch.

e. Trim close to the seam.

f. Turn and press.

Trim   Inside mitered corner

5. Shorten the unmitered corner on the machine just as it had been done originally.

6. Tack the hem up at the seamline.

7. Fold the lining up the amount you shortened the sleeve and press it.

8. Pin the mitered vent together.

9. Tack the lining to the sleeve.

10. Resew the buttons.

11. Press as described in "Shortening Sleeves without Vents."

*Note: If the sleeve is shortened so much that there is not enough fabric to make a vent, sew the vented seam together and shorten as if it were a sleeve with no vent.

Shortening Sleeves from the Top

    If the sleeves have some sort of decoration, cut buttonholes, etc., you may have to shorten them from the top. Refer to page 114 in the Blouse section for instructions. This is avoided if possible in coats because of the shoulder pads and lining. Sometimes the lining can still be shortened from the bottom by hand.

Shortening Raincoat Sleeves

    Raincoat sleeves take
a little longer to shorten
because they have tabs that
must be moved.

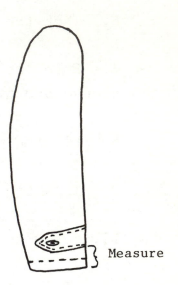

Measure

1. Mark the sleeve hem,
remembering to make it ½
to 1" longer than a blouse
or jacket sleeve.

2. Measure how far the tab
is from the original hem,
and move it up that distance
from the new hem. Do this
by going to the inside
through the sleeve lining
(instructions in "Shortening
Sleeves without Vents").
Rip the seam and move the
tab up the desired amount.

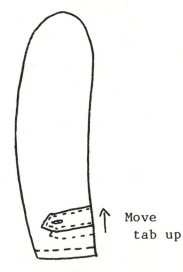

Move
tab up

3. Proceed with the sleeve
hem as for jackets and coats.

Lengthening Sleeves

Women's clothing almost never has enough fabric for lengthening sleeves. If you find that there is enough, follow the previous directions and lengthen where it says to shorten.

When adding a facing to sleeves, sometimes it is less bulky and looks better if you add to the lining rather than to the sleeve. It is easier to match the lining fabric than the outer fabric. If you do this, be sure to add interfacing to the bottom of the sleeve for more body.

If you are lengthening a sleeve all possible, you may have to take in the underarm seam at the bottom slightly. The sleeve has been made wider at the bottom so the hem will fit the sleeve when turned up.

Bottom of sleeve with hem let down all the way

After you have straightened the seam, you can do the hem by hand or attach the lining on the machine. Do this by opening a lining seam as described in "Shortening Sleeves without Vents."

Take in the seam so the hem doesn't fan out

In like manner, if you add
a facing to the sleeve, angle
it outward at the top so it
will fit when turned up. It's
best to use a bias facing and
very important not to stretch
it or the sleeve during application.

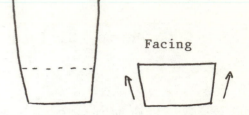

Facing

The sleeve angles outward
as it goes up, so angle
the facing outward too.

If the sleeve has a vent and mitered corner that has
been trimmed, you may not be able to lengthen the sleeve.
Be sure to advise the customer of this possibility before starting the alteration.

Narrowing Sleeves

If you are asked to narrow
jacket or coat sleeves,
remember they must fit over
other garments and still
have ease. Be sure to fit
the customer when she has on
other clothing she will be
wearing under the coat or
jacket. Alter according to
instructions in the "Dress"
chapter.

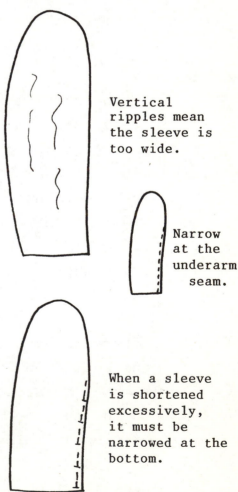

Vertical
ripples mean
the sleeve is
too wide.

Narrow
at the
underarm
seam.

When a sleeve
is shortened
excessively,
it must be
narrowed at the
bottom.

You may also have to narrow
a coat or jacket sleeve when
you have shortened it so
much the hem is very wide.
This is usually done from
the hem up to nothing at the
armhole.

Sideseams

Taking In

Taking in sideseams on a jacket or coat is just like taking in seams in any other garment. Pin, draw smooth alteration lines, sew, rip, and press. The only caution is against over fitting. Because jackets and coats are of heavier fabric, and other garments are worn under them, you must allow more ease for freedom of movement. Never sew the garment quite as tightly as you have fitted it (make seams about 1/8" less than marked).

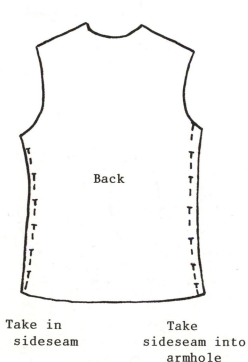

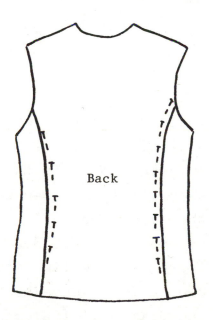

Take in   Take   Take in   Take side
sideseam   sideseam into side back   back seam into
                 armhole   seam   armhole

Sideseams into Armholes

When the seam needs to be
taken in all the way into
the armhole, you will have
to drop the armhole to com-
pensate.

Take sideseam into armhole

The natural tendency would
be to take in the sleeve to
fit the smaller armhole, but
this would make the sleeve
too tight.

Do not narrow sleeve seam

Instead, rip the bottom
half of the sleeve from the
armhole. Take in the sideseam first and then reapply
the sleeve on the new lower
sewing line. To determine
where the new line will be,
pin in the sleeve to see
where it will fit.

Trim the fabric from the armhole where you have dropped
it, or it will feel too tight.
Alter lining in the same way.

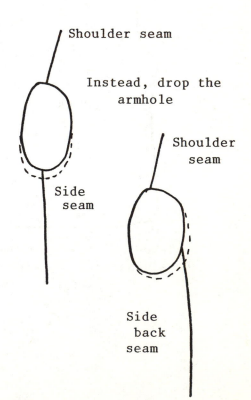

Shoulder seam

Instead, drop the
armhole

Shoulder
seam

Side
seam

Side
back
seam

Letting Out

Letting out sideseams on jackets and coats is the same as for other garments, depending on the availability of fabric.

If the garment is too tight, there will probably be pull lines, or the customer will not be able to close it in the front. Mark as for letting out, and be sure to let out the lining too.

Sometimes the body will fit well, but the customer will complain that it is too tight in the armholes, or too tight in the back (across the shoulders).

In this case, you would let
out the sideseams and the
sleeve seams. On the sleeve
seams, taper to nothing above
the elbow.

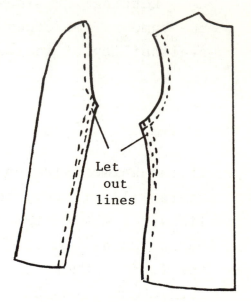

Let
out
lines

Sometimes there will be
large enough seams in the
outer fabric to let out,
but no seam allowance in
the lining. You will then
have to add a gusset to the
lining (instructions in the
"Blouse" chapter).

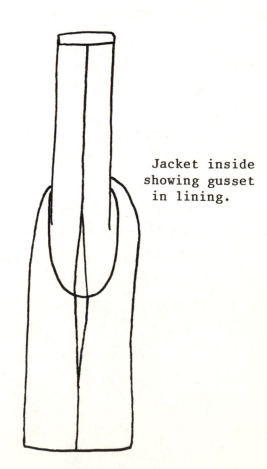

Jacket inside
showing gusset
in lining.

Darts

Taking in the Darts

If the jacket basically fits well, but needs more shape, you may be able to take in the vertical darts, or add some. For adding darts, see the "Blouse" chapter.

For taking in darts, pin at the widest part of the dart. This is all the fitting that is needed.

(This would be a good time to check the position of the dart points. Refer to the "Blouse" and "Dress" chapters for more dart discussion.)

Go to the inside and mark where the pin is holding the fabric. Use this as your widest mark and taper to nothing at the points.

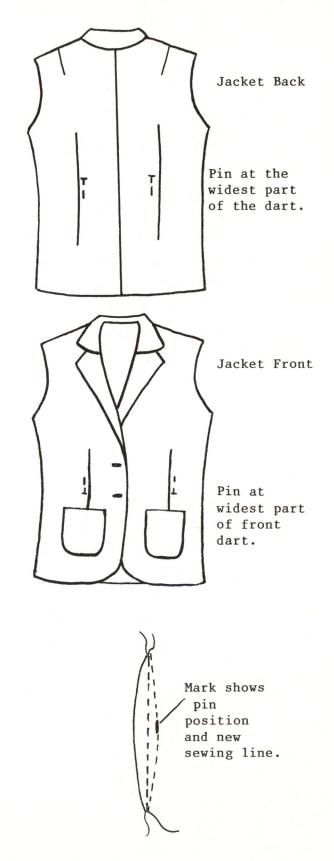

Jacket Back

Pin at the widest part of the dart.

Jacket Front

Pin at widest part of front dart.

Mark shows pin position and new sewing line.

If the dart is very wide, you
may have to trim it and press
it open so it won't pull.

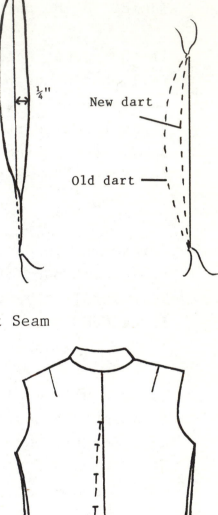

About 1½"

¼"

New dart

Old dart

Letting Darts Out

Darts can also be let out as a
last resort when all of the seams
have been let out all possible.
This can only be done if the old
stitching line doesn't show. It
is almost never done because the
fabric gained is minimal.

Taking in the Center Back Seam

The center back seam
should be taken in only when
the back needs more shaping.
Many alterationists make the
mistake of taking in the center back seam when they should
be taking in the sideseams.
This is used as a shortcut,
and a very bad one. When the
center back seam is taken in
instead of the sideseams, the
sideseams are pulled inward
and thrown off grain.

Sideseams are pulled inward
and off grain

The jacket should basically
fit well before the center
back seam is tapered. From
the side, the back will appear to have no curve.

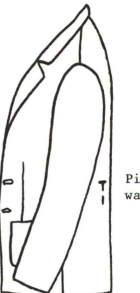

No
curve

Take a pinch of fabric at the
customer's waist and put a
pin in it.

Go to the inside and use the
pin mark as the widest part
of the seam. Taper to nothing
gradually.

Pin at
waist

You may have to trim and clip
the seam so it won't pull.

If the lining has a pleat in
the back, you do not need to
alter it.

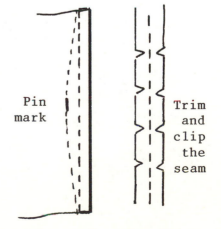

Pin
mark

Trim
and
clip
the
seam

Narrowing Shoulders

The shoulder seam in blouses usually comes right to the shoulder bone. Jacket shoulders extend ½ to 5/8" past the bone, and coats about an inch past the bone. This is to accommodate shoulder pads and the extra layers of clothing underneath.

Follow the directions for narrowing shoulders in the "Blouse" chapter. The only difference is that you may be working with shoulder pads and sleeve heads. Do one armhole at a time and reapply them the same way they were originally sewn in. Because of the thickness, attaching them by hand is usually the easiest way.

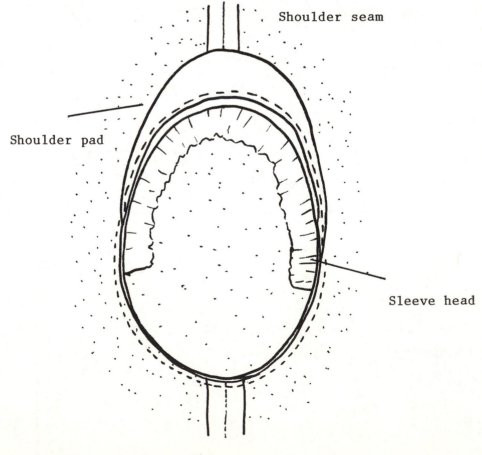

Shoulder seam

Shoulder pad

Sleeve head

Sideseam

There some extreme fashions where the shoulders are extended several inches beyond the body. The pads may be very thick also. If the customer wants the shoulders narrowed, it is best to remove the oversized pads first. Place a normal pad on the customer's shoulder underneath the garment and pin from there. You will probably have to drop the shoulder as well as narrow it, because extra fabric has been added for the pad.

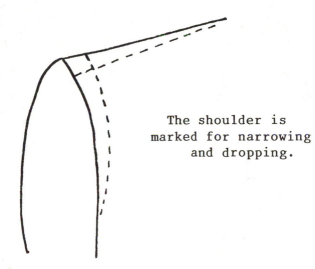

The shoulder is marked for narrowing and dropping.

When narrowing shoulders, the final pressing is very important. If you are going to be doing a lot of tailoring or alterations on coats and jackets, you should purchase a sleeve board so you will be able to press properly. If you do not have a sleeve board, roll up a towel or use a pressing ham to help simulate the shape of a shoulder and arm.

Shortening a Jacket

If you are asked to shorten a jacket, be sure to check the position of the pockets first. If the jacket is shortened a lot, the pockets may come too near the bottom and they will look out of place.

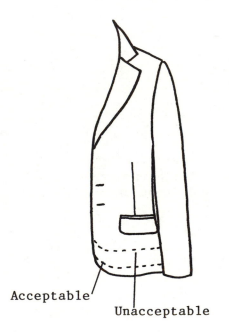

Acceptable
Unacceptable

Acceptable

Sometimes jackets with patch pockets will look all right if the jacket is shortened to the bottom of them. You will have to "eye ball" the look to see if it is acceptable. Patch pockets usually cannot be moved up because the old stitching lines will show.

If there is a pleat in the CB
and you shorten the jacket a
lot, the remaining pleat may
by very short. In this case,
you would close the pleat and
just have a normal seam.

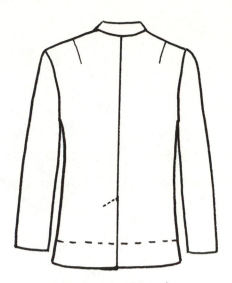

If the jacket is
shortened excessively,
close the vent.

1. Mark the new hemline all
around.

2. Detach the lining if there
is one, and rip the old hem
out.

3. If there is topstitching
on the CF, rip it out high
enough so it is out of your
work area.

4. Transfer the markings to
the inside. If the jacket is
curved in the front, turn the
facing inside out. Use one
side as a pattern to copy the
curve outline on the other
side.

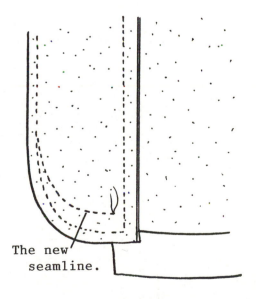

The new
seamline.

5. Sew the new curve and trim. To make a smooth curve, trim close to the edge with pinking shears.

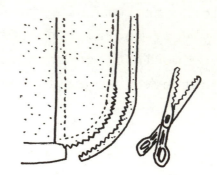

If the bottom is straight at the CF, do one side at a time and duplicate the way it was originally trimmed and pressed. To eliminate bulk at the bottom corners, trim close to the seams where the hem folds up. You can also stitch the ditch of the facing seam before the facing is folded back.

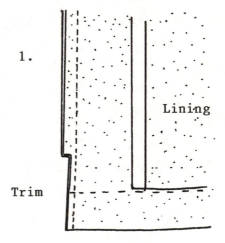

1.

Lining

Trim

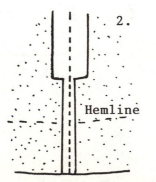

2.

Hemline

Facing seam open

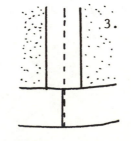

3.

Stitch the ditch

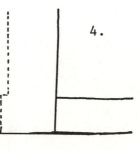

4.

Dotted lines show trimmed seamline underneath

There are several different
ways that the lining may
meet up with the bottom of
the facing. Use the ori-
ginal way it was done as
you

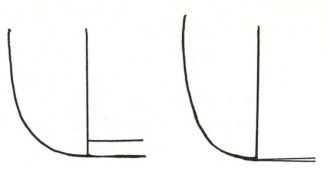

Lining up from hem   Lining flush

To make the lining flush
with the bottom, sew the
curve and stop 1" from the
edge of the facing.

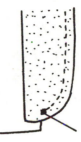

Sew to 1" from
the edge of the
facing

Sew the bottom of the lining
to the facing, right sides
together. Sew the lining as
far as it will go to the 1"
of facing that was left undone.

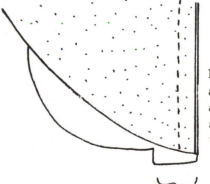

Lining
and facing
are right
sides
together

1"

Turn the 1" flap under. The
lining will automatically
turn under with it and will
be flush with the bottom.

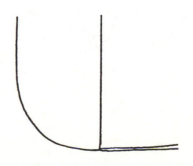

Lining is flush

If you want the lining to
stop above the hemline of
the jacket, turn the lining
up ½" before stitching it
to the facing. In this instance, you can sew the
facing curve all the way.

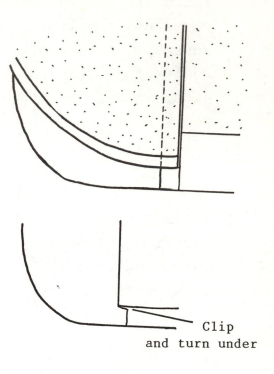

Turn the lining right side
out and press seams toward
the lining, except for the
facing that is below the
lining.

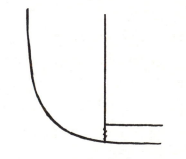

Clip
and turn under

Clip the facing at the bottom of the lining, and turn
the raw edge under. Tack it
in place.

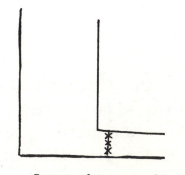

Tack in place

For coats, the fabric may be
too bulky to turn under.
Leave the raw edge and make
a small row of the tailor's
catch stitch ("Hand Sewing"
chapter) over it.

Cover the raw edge with
the tailor's catch
stitch

6. Turn the new hem up and press it. Move the interfacing up if necessary.

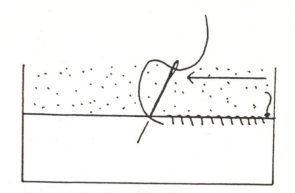

Whip stitch- sew from right to left

7. Sew the hem using one of the stitches described in the "Hand Sewing" chapter.

8. Turn the lining under and press it. Trim if there is more than 1" turned under. Always pin the lining down and check the outside to see if it is pulling.

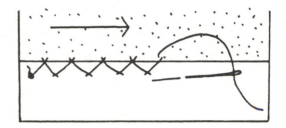

Catch stitch-sew from left to right

9. There should be some give or play at the bottom of the lining. Turn it up ¼" and tack it to the jacket with a running stitch.

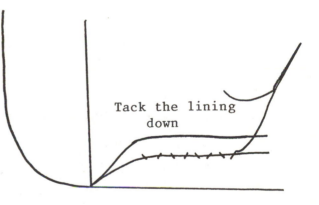

Tack the lining down

10. Press the hem and replace the topstitching. If you cannot match the thread in color or thickness, you may have to remove all the topstitching from the collar, lapels, and the CF edge. Then replace it all with the same thread.

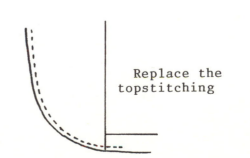

Replace the topstitching

167

Shortening a Coat

When fitting for a coat hem, ask the customer to wear her longest street length dress under it. Coats are usually 1 to 1½" longer than dresses. Remember to make the hem a little longer in back (see "Skirt Hems").

After you have marked the hem all around, study the hem and lining to see how they are sewn and attached to each other. Take notes or draw a little diagram if necessary. The coat itself will be your guide. Try to duplicate the original hemming method as closely as possible.

This is always the best policy to follow because there are so many different techniques in hemming coats. If you learn only one way, you will be unable to complete a job when it is different.

Go to the "Shortening a Jacket" section and study it. There are various techniques for attaching the lining at the bottom of the facing.

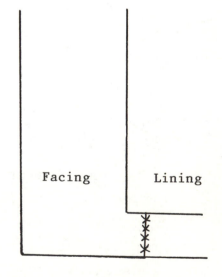

Facing   Lining

If the lining is free hanging,
it may be attached with tailor's
tacks or thread chains to the
coat. Instructions for these
are in the "Hand Sewing" chapter.

Instructions for attaching
lining to a pleat edge are in
the "Skirt" chapter.

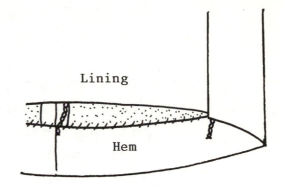

Tailor's tacks hold lining
to hem

One problem you may encounter with coats is in
pressing. Coat fabrics are usually thick and many have
a nap that can become flattened when pressed. To avoid
this, always use a press cloth. If you do flatten the
nap, hold the iron just above the fabric and steam it.
This may lift the nap. If not, steam the fabric and
gently rub it on itself. This almost always helps to
restore the nap.

Steam to
raise the nap

Shortening a Raincoat

As with coats, there are many different hemming styles or techniques, and you will need to duplicate the original one.

Raincoat hems are almost always topstitched, and matching the thread can be very difficult. Advise the customer that she may have to just settle for the best possible match.

Since the hems are topstitched, take special time in fitting to make sure the length is correct. Raincoat hems are 1 to 2" below the street length of dresses or skirts. This is so the coat will be able to protect the clothing from the elements.

Be careful when marking. Wax chalk almost always leaves a grease mark on raincoat fabric, and pins quite often leave permanent holes. A light mark with real chalk is the best.

A raincoat hem is one of the few hems that is folded over twice and topstitched. Always give the hem a good press before sewing. Raincoat fabric does not ease in well. If you find that there is excess fabric which does not allow the hem to lie flat, you may need to take in each seam below the hemline.

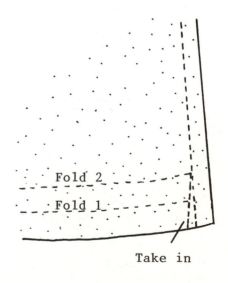

To reduce bulk at the front corners, you can trim the facing corner before sewing.

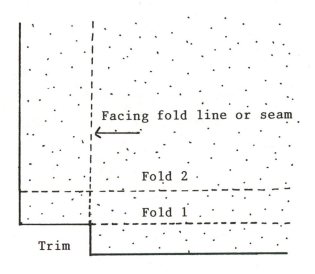

Facing fold line or seam

Fold 2

Fold 1

Trim

Some raincoats will be made of a plastic or coated fabric. Never touch them with an iron or they will melt. I would even avoid using a press cloth because the plastics can shrink or melt with very little heat. Pins will leave holes. Use basting tape, fabric glue, or simply "hand press" a crease before sewing.

Review "Shortening a Jacket" for other hemming details. Also see the "Skirt" chapter for attaching lining to a pleat.

Shortening a Leather Coat

I will first of all caution you against doing any leather work unless you are a fairly accomplished sewer. Have leather needles and heavy duty thread and practice on leather scraps before you alter a customer's garment.

You will need to mark hems for leather coats with clothespins or clips.

The original hem will either be topstitched or glued, or both. If there is no topstitching, it has been glued and you will need to soften the glue. Do this carefully with a dry iron and press cloth. Touch the garment with the iron only long enough to warm the leather. Gently pull the old hem open, a small amount at a time.

When the hem is topstitched, remove the topstitching. If the threads are very hard to pull out, the hem is glued too. You will have to soften the glue and rip the threads alternating each step.

Mark the new hem on the inside with chalk. Turn it up and trim off the excess. Use this for practice in topstitching so you can get the correct length and tension.

If there is no topstitching, apply glue or rubber cement to the hem and coat. Allow it to become tacky and press the hem up with your hand. Hold it in place with your hand, a book, or a tailor's clapper until set.

Shorten the lining just as we did in jackets and coats.

Lengthening Jackets or Coats

Before promising to lengthen a jacket or coat, check to see if it has been trimmed in the front by the facing. If so, it cannot be lengthened. Also, if the garment is curved in front, it cannot be lengthened because the curve cannot be let out.

If you are lengthening all possible and adding a facing, always use a wide bias facing. Refer to "Pants" and "Skirts" chapters for details on facings. With coats, you may have to face the lining hem too.

Relining Jackets and Coats

The lining in jackets and coats almost always wears out before the garment itself does. For this reason, you will be asked to reline them.

Remove the old lining and gently rip it apart to use as a pattern. Put marks where seams are attached to each other. Press the original pieces, trying not to stretch them out of shape. Refer to "Replacing Lining in Pants" for the steps in this process.

Always discuss beforehand what fabric the customer wants. You may have to request a few alternates if you cannot find the exact one that she desires.

Interlining Coats

It is sometimes necessary in very cold climates to add interlining to coats.

This can be done in two ways. The first is to add a complete second lining using the original lining as a pattern. Fabric such as flannel or lightweight wool is used. The interlining is inserted between the lining and the coat.

The second way is to add a partial back interlining similar to the back interfacing in jackets and coats. Draw a pattern from the coat itself and insert the interlining tacking it to the shoulder seams, back armholes, neckline, and sides. It hangs freely at the bottom.

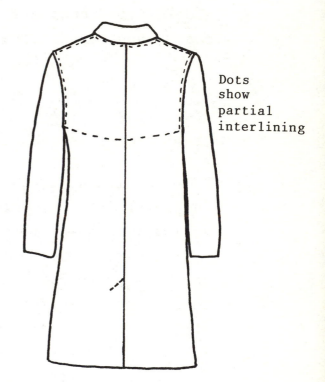

Dots show partial interlining

It is best to use a soft fabric, or to cut the whole piece on the bias so it will fall smoothly over the back. I have even seen a piece of chamois leather used for this purpose.

Before interlining any coat, be sure that there is enough fitting ease to allow for an added layer of fabric.

Narrowing Lapels

The width of lapels is determined by personal taste
and by style. When lapels
are narrowed, the collar is
usually cut back the same
amount. Every jacket is
different, and if the lapels
are narrowed only slightly,
the collar may not need to
be cut back. This is mostly
up to how the area looks by
eyeballing it. Usually the
lapel notch and the collar
width are the same measurement when done.

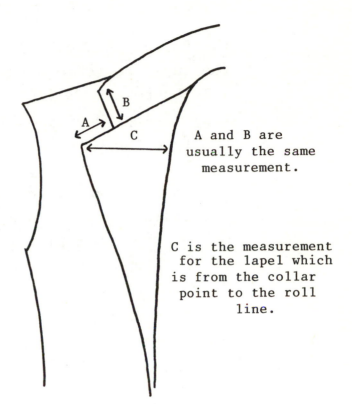

A and B are
usually the same
measurement.

C is the measurement
for the lapel which
is from the collar
point to the roll
line.

1. Measure the lapel and
collar and determine how
much each is to be narrowed.
Draw a line where the finished edges will be.

2. Remove the topstitching
from the collar and lapels.

3. Rip the lining out at
the bottom of the jacket.

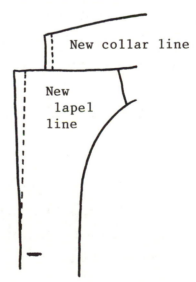

New collar line

New
lapel
line

4. On the inside, rip the collar far enough off of the lapel so you can narrow each edge. Some collars will be sewn just like a blouse collar, and others will be applied by attaching the under collar first, and then the upper collar and lapels.

5. Turn enough of the collar inside out so you can narrow it. When pivoting at the corner, take 1 or 2 diagonal stitches over it and meet up with the original sewing line.

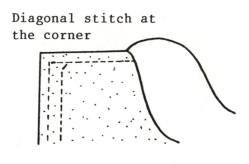

Diagonal stitch at the corner

Results with diagonal stitch

Results when sewn normally

6. Trim to ¼" from the sewing line and diagonally over the corners.

7. Turn and press.

8. Turn the lapels inside out and mark the new sewing line. Taper to nothing at the roll line.

9. Sew from the roll line
up, pivot with a diagonal
stitch at the corner. After
pivoting at the corner, sew
a slightly convex (curving
upward) line rather than
straight. When turned right
side out, this will prevent
a dip in the notch. Sew
across the neckline so the
collar is attached.

10. Trim the seam to ¼" and
diagonally over the corner.

11. Turn right side out and
press. Always press on the
under side of the collar and
lapels to prevent scorching.
This will also help the collar and lapels to roll back.

12. Replace the topstitching.
Start at the roll line and
go up. Pivot at the lapel
point and at the collar.
Stitch the ditch at the neckline seam and then pivot upward to the collar.

13. Do a final press.

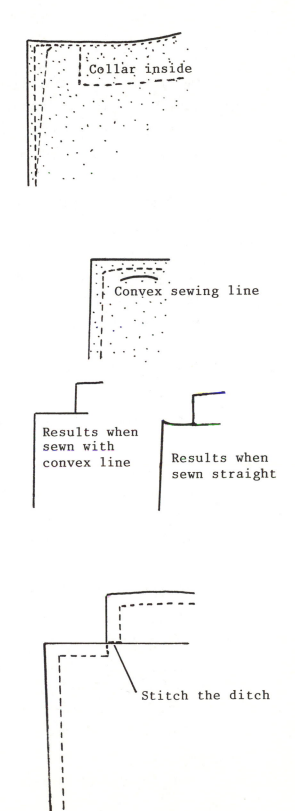

Collar inside

Convex sewing line

Results when
sewn with
convex line

Results when
sewn straight

Stitch the ditch

177

You may occasionally be
asked to add an inside chest
pocket to a jacket. The
pocket is usually put inside
the left side, but ask the
customer her preference.

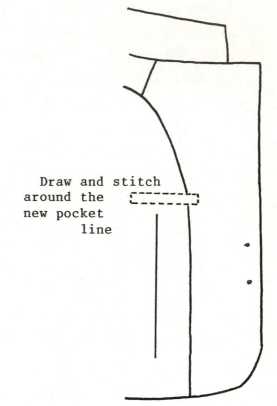

**Draw and stitch
around the
new pocket
line**

1. Go to the inside and
draw an oblong box ½" x 4",
or whatever width the customer wants. The pocket
location is just above the
vertical dart point and it
extends ½" into the facing.

2. Rip the lining from the
bottom of the jacket so you
can have access to the pocket
area. Stitch around the box
that you marked to stabilize
it.

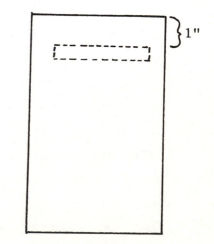

3. Cut a piece of lining
fabric 5" x 10". On it, draw
a box 4" x ½" in chalk. Make
the top line of the box 1"
down from the top of the fabric.

4. Put the pocket fabric on top of the jacket, lining up the boxes. Stitch around the box with small stitches.

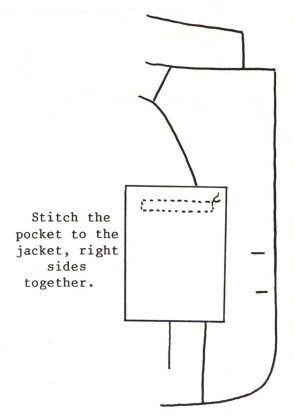

Stitch the pocket to the jacket, right sides together.

5. Slash down the middle of the box and diagonally to the corners.

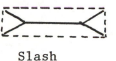

Slash

6. Turn the pocket to the inside. Let the fabric cover the raw edges of the slashed box. This will form "fake" welts for the pocket opening. Topstitch around the edge of the pocket opening.

Topstitch around the pocket opening

7. On the inside, fold the pocket in half and match the top edges. Stitch together across the top and then stitch the sides.

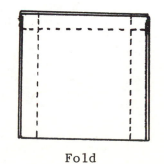

Fold

8. Tack the lining back to the jacket at the bottom.

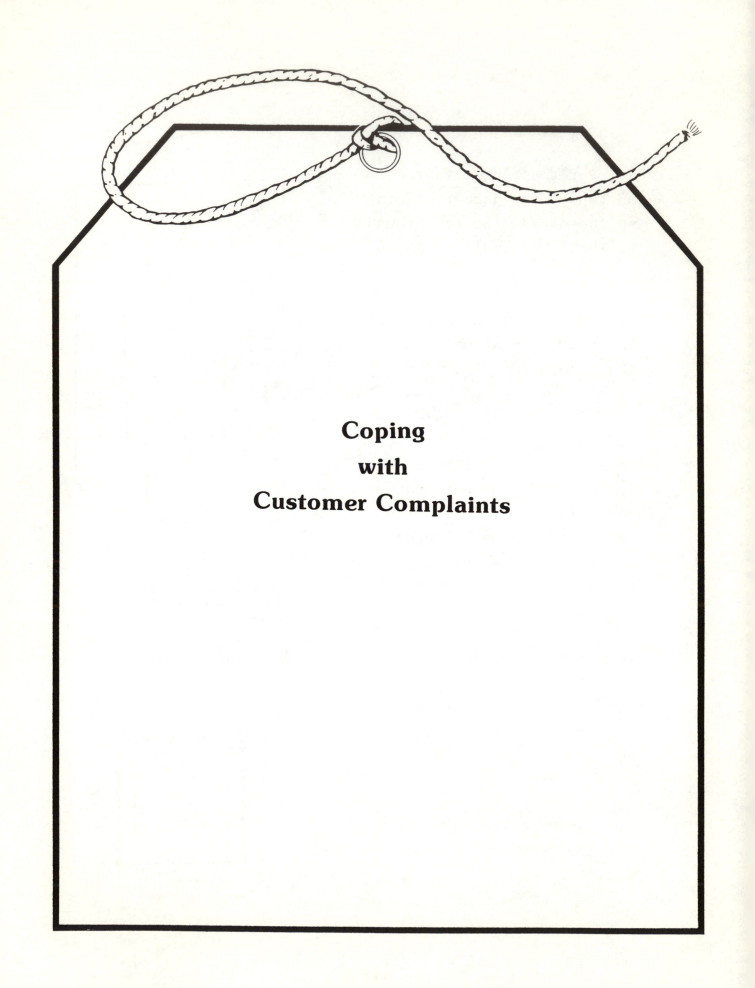

Coping

with

Customer Complaints

No matter how reputable the business, an occasional customer complaint is unavoidable. Following are some tips that will help in this area:

* __Always do the best possible work.__ If you have fulfilled your end of the bargain, there will be very few reasons for complaints.

* Make sure the customer tries the garment on when she comes to pick it up. Then you will be sure she is satisfied and that she feels your work is acceptable.

* Keep accurate records of everything. You may need to refer back to them. Describe in detail the specifications for the job and write them down. Make note of and date any changes that the customer may make over the phone.

* At your first meeting, specify time limits for redos and charges for the same if there are any. For instance, you will make changes free of charge for the first month and will charge after that. Decide on your return policies and write them on your receipt.

* Always be professional and businesslike with customers no matter how friendly you become with them. Give receipts for everything, even for work redone or done free.

* Never admit guilt on the phone. First
  of all, if you have done your best work,
  there will be a very slim chance that the
  complaint is legitimate. Secondly, you
  have no control over what happens to the
  garment when it leaves your place of business, so reserve comment until you see
  it. Say you are sorry there is a problem
  and ask when would be a convenient time
  to get together.

* Always remain calm, even if the customer
  isn't. If the complaint turns out to be
  a legitimate one, fix it cheerfully. Examples of illegitimate complaints would
  be wanting a style change after explicitly
  requesting the one she has, wanting a hem
  change after not bringing the proper shoes
  to the fitting, wanting free alterations
  after gaining or losing weight, etc. If
  the customer is wrong, try not to be ac-
  cusing or sarcastic. By referring to the
  receipt or business contract, you should
  easily be able to find who is in error
  without pointing a finger. Most problems
  arise out of misunderstandings and can be
  solved without ill feelings.

In general, when dealing with customers, present
yourself as a professional. Keep your personal life
out of the conversation and try to keep the subject on
business. Be courteous and remember that customers
will return if they have had a pleasant experience.

Suggested Price List

The following price list has been compiled over the last fifteen years from price lists nationwide. It is meant to be used as a guide and should be adjusted according to your location, your skill level, and your experience. You should revise your prices at least once a year. The best price list is one that you feel comfortable with and that is profitable for you. There will always be jobs that will be difficult to quote a set price for. I recommend that you charge by the hour for those.

Pants

Hem- shorten or lengthen................. $3.00-10.00
   lined .... add 2.00
   cuffs .... add 2.00
   levis 5.00-8.00
   face .... add 3.00
   with zippers................................ add 3.00

Sideseams- in or out 5.00-7.50
   lined .... add 4.00
   pockets .... add 5.00

Waist- in or out 6.50
   remove waistband 10.00
   levis 9.00

Seat only- in or out 4.00

Drop waistband 12.00
   move zipper 15.00

Waist, Seat, and Stride 10.00
   lined .... add 5.00

Crotch adjustment............................. 5.00
   lined .... add 2.00
   crotchpiece 7.50

Tapering legs 10.00
   lined 15.00

Pants continued-

Replace zipper 6.50
    levis 8.00

Put in lining 17.50

Skirts

Hem- shorten or lengthen 7.50-25.00
    lined .... add 3.00
    face 10.00-30.00
    with pleat .... add 2.00
    topstitched .... add 3.00
    wedding gown 15.00-45.00
        with train .... add 10.00
        shorten from waist 15.00
        move zipper down .... add 5.00

Waist and sides- in or out .... same as for pants

Sides in through hem or narrow skirt 10.00
    lined .... add 3.00

Drop waistband .... same as for pants

Protruding hip bones 6.00

High hip 6.00

Put in lining 15.00

Replace zipper 7.50

Replace elastic in waist 6.00

Blouses

Narrow shoulders 8.00

Drop shoulders (sloping shoulders) 6.00
    drop armhole .... add 4.00

Erect shoulders 6.00

Add back darts 4.00

Blouses continued-

Add bust darts 6.00

Sides in 6.00
  flat felled seams .... add 6.00

Gussets 8.50

Shortening sleeves 6.00
  move placket .... add 2.00
  from top 10.00
Shorten blouse 5.00
  curved hem .... add 1.00

Narrow collar 6.00

Replace neckline zipper in a knit 7.50

Dresses

Shorten bodice (take out blouson) 10.00

Lengthen bodice (short waisted) 11.00

Reposition bust darts 4.00

Sway back 10.00

Take in back 6.00

Dowager's hump (neck darts) 4.00
  front adjustment 12.00

High hip and low shoulder 15.00

Add shoulder pads 5.00
  remove 2.00

Take in (narrow) or let out sleeves 5.00
  gussets 8.50

Change sleeve pitch 8.00

Jackets and Coats

Sleeves- lengthen or shorten 5.00
  lined 6.50
  with vents .... add 2.50
  face .... add 3.00
  raincoat 6.50
    move tab .... add 2.00
  narrow 8.00
    lined .... add 4.00
  shorten from top 15.00
Sideseams- in or out 6.00
  lined 8.00
  through armhole 10.00
    lined 12.00
  add gusset to lining .... add 4.00

Darts- in or out 3.50
  lined 5.00

Take in center back seam 4.00
  lined 6.00

Narrow shoulders 10.00
  lined 15.00

Put in shoulder pads 6.00
  remove pads 4.00

Hem- lengthen or shorten
  Jacket 10.00
    lined 15.00
  Coat 12.50
    lined 17.50
  Raincoat 15.00
  Leather 20.00

  Lengthen and add facing to any of the above- 5.00

Reline .... 25.00 plus fabric
Add interlining to coats .... 35.00 plus fabric
  Partial interlining .... 20.00 plus fabric

Narrow lapels 25.00

Add inside pocket 6.00

Index

Other Books by Mary Roehr

Speed Tailoring is a completely illustrated spiral-bound book telling the fastest and easiest way to construct a woman's lined blazer. It includes instructions on the use of fusibles, machine shoulder pad application, professional collar and lapel placement (as done in ready-to-wear), cutting, finishing, pressing methods, bound buttonholes, patch, flap, and bound pockets, pressing methods, and more. $12.95

Sewing As A Home Business tells how to start and operate a sewing business in your home. It includes licensing, taxes, advertising, customer relations, target markets, bookkeeping, and advice to spouses. There are complete price lists for custom sewing and alterations for men and women, and discussion on how to figure an hourly rate. If you have a sewing machine, you will be able to start a profitable business now! $11.95

Altering Men's Ready-to-Wear is 150 pages with hundreds of illustrations. Pictures show how to identify the problem and what to do to correct it. Included are pants, shirts, jackets, coats, vests, and neckties. Marking, pressing, hand sewing, and prices for men's alterations are there too. A handy index will help you locate the solution to your problem quickly. If you have wanted to alter men's clothing, now is the time to start! $14.95

Altering Women's Ready-to-Wear $17.95

For ordering or quantity information:
Mary Roehr Custom Tailoring, 3885 Lakemont Dr., Memphis, Tennessee, 38128. Check, Money Order, VISA, Mastercard.
    *Please add $1.00 per total order for postage.